Style and Statistics

Wiley & SAS Business Series

The Wiley & SAS Business Series presents books that help senior-level managers with their critical management decisions.

Titles in the Wiley & SAS Business Series include:

Analytics in a Big Data World: The Essential Guide to Data Science and Its Applications by Bart Baesens

Bank Fraud: Using Technology to Combat Losses by Revathi Subramanian

Big Data Analytics: Turning Big Data into Big Money by Frank Ohlhorst

Big Data, Big Innovation: Enabling Competitive Differentiation through Business Analytics by Evan Stubbs

Business Analytics for Customer Intelligence by Gert Laursen

Business Intelligence Applied: Implementing an Effective Information and Communications Technology Infrastructure by Michael Gendron

Business Intelligence and the Cloud: Strategic Implementation Guide by Michael S. Gendron

Business Transformation: A Roadmap for Maximizing Organizational Insights by Aiman Zeid

Connecting Organizational Silos: Taking Knowledge Flow Management to the Next Level with Social Media by Frank Leistner

Data-Driven Healthcare: How Analytics and BI Are Transforming the Industry by Laura Madsen

Delivering Business Analytics: Practical Guidelines for Best Practice by Evan Stubbs

Demand-Driven Forecasting: A Structured Approach to Forecasting, Second Edition by Charles Chase

Demand-Driven Inventory Optimization and Replenishment: Creating a More Efficient Supply Chain by Robert A. Davis

Developing Human Capital: Using Analytics to Plan and Optimize Your Learning and Development Investments by Gene Pease, Barbara Beresford, and Lew Walker

The Executive's Guide to Enterprise Social Media Strategy: How Social Networks Are Radically Transforming Your Business by David Thomas and Mike Barlow

The Value of Business Analytics: Identifying the Path to Profitability by Evan Stubbs

The Visual Organization: Data Visualization, Big Data, and the Quest for Better Decisions by Phil Simon

Too Big to Ignore: The Business Case for Big Data by Phil Simon

Using Big Data Analytics: Turning Big Data into Big Money by Jared Dean

Win with Advanced Business Analytics: Creating Business Value from Your Data by Jean Paul Isson and Jesse Harriott

For more information on any of the above titles, please visit www.wiley.com.

Style and Statistics

The Art of Retail Analytics

Brittany Bullard

WILEY

Contents

Acknowledgments

Thank you to all those who helped me get to where I am today. I'd like to thank the Retail Analytics team for contributing to the overall vision of retail: Lori Schafer, Dan Mitchell, Andrew Fowkes, Kevin Mac-Donald, Jason Gautereaux, and Colin Reid. I want to thank Elizabeth Dove, Donna McGuckin, Jeff Thomas, Susan Carol, Charlie Chase, and Lauren Case for reviewing my manuscript. Their review and feedback have enhanced the quality of this book, and I greatly appreciate their efforts. Thank you to my amazing editor, Stacey Hamilton. I also want to thank my management: Gene Gsell, Greg Soussloff, Sandy Defelice, and Jason Gautereaux for supporting my endeavors.

Shout-out to my SAS Professional Services team and the Beall's family for shaping me into the retailer I am today: Steve Knopik, Lorna Nagler, Thomas Williams, Victor D'Amato, Ron Friese, Pam Meyer, Kerri Devine, Ann Ferguson, Scott Langford, Kristen Henrichs, and Phillip Wozny.

Most important, thank you to my family for supporting me throughout the process. Thank you to my son, Landon Bullard, for dealing with some weekends stuck in the house. Biggest thanks to my other half, Nick Berg, for constantly being there for me along the way and pushing me to finish.

About the Author

Brittany Bullard is a Solutions and Analytical Consultant in the Retail and Consumer Packaged Goods Practice at SAS Institute. Bullard focuses on retailers' strategic problems and identifies the challenges they face in an evolving industry. Her role allows her to apply her knowledge of advanced analytics to solve the most pressing issues and position SAS's customers for success.

Bullard brings to her team a decade of experience in the retail industry and a fresh millennial perspective on the customer and user experience. Versed in retail forecasting and omnichannel analytics, she serves as a member of the Strategic Retail Analytics team at SAS and on the Global Retail Community of Industry Leaders as the representative for the United States.

Originally a chemistry and math fiend, Bullard found the application of analytics in retail a perfect union of her strengths and passions. She now works to educate others on how they can drive innovation and develop professionally by leveraging the power of analytics.

Prior to joining SAS, Bullard acted as the manager of Forecasting, Allocation, and Replenishment at Beall's Inc. Her leadership of the implementation and management of retail analytics at Beall's connected Bullard to the SAS retail team. Bullard collaborates on the design of retail-focused solutions and the SAS Assortment Management portfolio, which was recognized as a leader in the Forrester Wave in 2014 and the Gartner Magic Quadrant in 2014, 2015, and 2016.

Introduction

Have you ever walked into a department store and wondered how the magic of sights, smells, and staging came together? The sweet smell of gardenia wafting from the fragrance department; the eclectic assortment of pumps, sandals, and flats in the shoe department; and the eye-catching visual merchandising of in-season colors and fashions that captures the essence of time? Such is the life of a retailer, who blends art and science to create an environment where you, the shopper, take center stage.

Many major retailers started out as individually owned stores. The owners ran the store themselves. They were in the store day in and day out so they knew their business. They knew their customers and their customers' preferences. Pricing of products was a pretty basic concept. The owners marketed by word of mouth or through local flyers and newspapers. Successful owners were able to add on more locations. As location growth increased, the complexity of buying, planning, and marketing increased. No longer were the owners in each location every day, nor did they know all of their customers on a first-name basis. With this expansion, retailers understood their customers less and were unable to tackle the workload on their own. Marketing became more difficult as well. The sheer volume of work became increasingly larger as businesses grew.

Therefore, owners began to hire a staff, who became an essential piece of the puzzle. Buyers or merchants were responsible for picking out products, determining how much to buy from different vendors, planning sales, planning inventory, and advertising their goods. The buyer had many functions in the beginning. Buyers tend to be individuals with a great eye for design. They are usually very artistic and creative individuals with good taste. Sometimes these individuals are described as being right-brained. The right side of the brain controls tasks that have to do with creativity and artistry. The right-brained, creative element for a merchant is a key benefit for selecting the perfect merchandise.

But eventually it became clear that businesses also needed a "left-brained" perspective to ensure profitability through math and logic. The left side of the brain controls tasks that have to do with logic. The left side is more geared toward math and science. Over time, the Picasso-Einstein model developed. Buyers are the Picassos, who are in charge of fashion artistry. Planners are the Einsteins, ensuring maximum profitability through math and science.

The original buyer's role of picking products, determining how much to buy, planning sales, monitoring inventory, and managing other key metrics was divided up. Although the roles vary by retailer, in general, the planner manages the financial aspect of the business, ensuring that the sales targets are planned along with other key performance indicators and inventory. The merchant or buyer controls the selection and management of the assortment, within the financial budget that has been established by the planner. The buyer has the eye for fashion, trends, and taste. The planner ensures that the financial and strategic targets are achieved.

The greatest performance comes from a perfect marriage of the two roles. If planners were in charge of both roles, they would likely never take risks, have incredibly low inventories, and probably sacrifice presentation standards for fear of wasted inventory. Together, this partnership creates a beautiful, profitable business. The perfect marriage of art and science, it later evolved to the art and analytics of retail.

Marketing has evolved over time as well. Marketing developed from advertising. Today, advertising is a component of marketing. Advertising includes spreading the word about your brand or business. With most businesses, advertising begins as word of mouth. It can then branch out to newspaper ads, magazine ads, and even social media! Brands and retailers are now advertising on a plethora of platforms. The creation and nurturing of a retail brand is its lifeblood; think of Williams-Sonoma or Nordstrom; they both have a "brand" identity that invites and nurtures loyal customers. These brands reach their target audience through buying specific market ads to truly connect to their customers and sustain this brand loyalty.

But advertising is only one component of marketing. Marketing is the overall strategic planning, execution, and measuring of how a retailer or a brand interacts with its customers and how that brand is perceived. Public relations and community involvement aid in brand perception. Marketing is no longer thought of as a commercial or a newspaper ad. Instead, it is thought of as a lifetime relationship between a brand and a customer.

There are multiple components of a retailer's business. These components have historically worked in silos. Merchandising and marketing, as described earlier, are two key components to driving merchandise assortments and communicating the most relevant information in the most effective way to the customer. The in-store teams, or store operations, are the components of the business that interact with the customers. The in-store teams are at the forefront of building relationships with customers once the merchandising, pricing, and marketing strategies have been executed. Last, cybersecurity is the component of the business that protects customers against cyberattacks and ensures that personal information, including credit card data, is not compromised.

The retail environment has had significant changes over the last couple of years with the rise of the digital landscape, an increase in e-commerce business, and the rise of the millennial customer. For retailers to be successful, they must break down the silos of these different components to their business to truly understand and shape the customer journey. In this book, we will walk through each component of the retailer's business. We will discuss what each component is responsible for, how retailers are able to intertwine the components, the challenges retailers face, and how retailers can leverage analytics to overcome challenges while maintaining the art of retail to drive profitability and efficiencies.

CHAPTER **1**

The Changing
Face of Retail

The Internet completely transformed the retail industry and the way we think about shopping. Retail changed from walking through a store to a click of a button while sitting on your couch in your yoga pants. The growth of mobile and technology has also revolutionized the industry.

The first online retail site was created in 1979. Michael Aldrich connected a television to a computer that processed transactions in real time using a telephone. He called it Videotex. This was even before the World Wide Web. Tim Berners-Lee created the first World Wide Web server in 1990. The first retail site was a book retailer, www.books.com. In 1994, a secure port was developed for online transactions. This meant that customers were able to purchase items online through a relatively safe process, avoiding fraud and identity theft. It was by no means 100% secure, but it was better than previous attempts. Still, people were somewhat skeptical about making purchases online.

Amazon and eBay quickly followed in 1995. I remember surfing for designer items on eBay in my younger years. I had somewhat of an obsession with Nancy Kerrigan during my childhood. My first eBay/online purchase was a Nancy Kerrigan refrigerator magnet. When it arrived, I discovered that it was literally a cut-out of Nancy Kerrigan from a magazine article, laminated, with a magnet glued to the back.

That was the risk you faced during eBay's early years of bidding on items. Then eBay transformed into more structure and reliability. A "buy" option was also implemented, rather than waiting to be outbid or win. I'm not going to lie: I enjoyed the rush of the bidding process and the not knowing what you were going to receive in the mail. This might have been due to my age, but it created great memories.

Amazon was also one of the first e-retailers that only sold online. It has now grown to be the largest e-commerce retailer and recently opened a physical store location. Amazon started out selling books and has now grown to sell clothing, electronics, home goods, and even food. Amazon Prime offers free two-day shipping, which has attracted a vast audience. Amazon has also started same-day delivery in select major cities with a new program called AmazonFresh. Amazon's latest technological move is the dash button, a small button that can stick to any surface and connects to a customer's Amazon

Prime account and Wi-Fi. When the button is pressed, it sends an order to Amazon. These dash buttons are available for brands such as Cottonelle, Clorox, Dasani, Red Bull, Tide, and many more common household products. If a customer notices she is running low on toilet paper, a simple click of the dash button generates an order, and a box of toilet paper is delivered to her door in two days. Amazon is becoming the king of e-commerce in today's market and will reach 19% of market share by 2020, making Amazon the largest retailer in the world.

The evolving technologies have changed not only the way we think of shopping but also our expectations. "Millennials" is a term used to describe people who were born between the years 1982 and 2004. This generation has predominantly grown up during the age of technology. A millennial's first job was after the BlackBerry and Internet were invented. Technology is a known way of life to them. The millennials are a technology-savvy generation. Education has incorporated technology as a staple in their development. Therefore, millennials have much higher expectations from retailers.

I myself am a millennial. I remember the launch of AOL; online dating when it was in the form of chatrooms; and MTV when it was actually videos with my boy Carson Daly, and you were not cool if you didn't have a cell phone in middle school. These expectations are even greater for the younger spectrum of millennials.

We check our phone on average 45 times per day and spend 3.2 hours on our mobile devices. Social media is a large part of a millennial's life. Social media is the means by which we communicate and stay informed with what is going on in the news. The first social media sites were Myspace in 2003 and Facebook in 2004. Myspace is an online community that slowly lost popularity over the years. It is still around but has become more of an avenue for musicians. Facebook started as a social community only for individuals with a university e-mail address. It slowly evolved to include community colleges and eventually opened to the public, moving from exclusively college students to everyone and their grandmother.

In 2014, Facebook had 1.23 billion monthly active users. As Facebook grew, so did other social sites, such as Instagram, which is a site where individuals share pictures. This site came on the scene in 2010.

In 2014, Instagram had 300 million active members. Twitter came on the scene in 2006 with the concept of leveraging Facebook's statuses and through it emerged the infamous hashtags. Hashtags are now a part of the millennial English language. A hashtag is a word or phrase that describes a topic, an event, or a person. These words or phrases begin with a hash or pound mark.

For example, #ThrowbackThursday is a hashtag used on social sites every Thursday where individuals post old pictures of themselves. Hashtags are used for searching on Twitter and Instagram. I have a good friend who has a weird obsession with cats. I think we all know a few of these people. She frequently searches #cats, so the content on her homepage has been tailored to show things of interest to her, such as cats. Tagging your picture with the #cats description will increase the likelihood that your picture will show up on her page and she will like it. Liking is a whole other concept. On any social site, people are able to click "Like" on your picture. It is almost a personal mission to try to get the most likes. Timing is involved in this as well. A millennial typically will not post his or her best pictures on a Saturday night at 10 pm because that's when everyone is out. If you post your best pictures with a large number of hashtags on a Monday around 4 pm when the workday is nearly over, your "like" factor will skyrocket.

Snapchat started in September 2011 and has evolved to be the second-most used social media app among millennials. Snapchat is a mobile app that allows you to take pictures, selfies, or videos and send them to select individuals or post to "your story." The kicker is that if you send the pictures or videos to an individual, the picture expires after 10 seconds, and only one replay is allowed per day. This app also enables users to send text messages that disappear after they have been read. If someone takes a screenshot of the picture, the app will actually tell the sender. This is of great appeal to any young millennials who do not want to leave a trail.

It is important to understand these different social media apps and how they work to best target and understand customers. Social media is a growing platform for retailers to reach their target audience. When it comes to social media sites, millennials start using these sites first, and then they slowly grow to reach the masses. This is why it is so important to understand millennials. There is a lot of hype in the market that if people are only focusing on millennials, then they are thinking that there are only jellyfish in the ocean. But the truth is, millennials lead the pack in expectations of retailers' technological capabilities and social presence. Once millennials' expectations come to fruition in the mainstream market, they tend to become the expectations of all generations. #Trendsetters is the hashtag that would describe this phenomenon. Social media began as a millennial fad but is now an all-generation fad. As a result, social media has become a critical element to reaching customers of all ages.

Social media sites also have influence on retailer websites. Take, for example, the app Tinder. Tinder is a dating app where people create a profile with information about themselves as well as a couple of pictures. If you are not interested in a profile that appears, you swipe to the right. If you swipe to the left, then you are interested and the app shows additional profiles of individuals who you may be interested in. If you would like to see more pictures of the person, then you swipe up and down to move through pictures. If you swipe to the left and the other person swipes to the left, then you both are able to communicate with each other through messaging. This is ideal in the social dating world because it reduces the number of people who you are not interested in messaging you. I only know all of this from a friend, of course, and you may be wondering what in the world this has to do with retail. I don't blame you. This style of app is actually influencing the way retailers change the design of their mobile sites. The best websites, software, and processes are ones that tie to how an individual is accustomed to performing a task or workflow.

Forever 21 is a fashion retailer geared toward millennials. The company has redesigned its mobile app to reflect this same type of style. You swipe to the left to see additional products, and you swipe up and down to see more pictures of the product in different angles. It's genius. It is all about creating a process that already ties to someone's habits. That is how you create a great customer experience. Ease of use and customer experience help drive customers to purchase as well as create strong customer loyalty.

"Channel" is a term retailers use to describe the mechanism through which customers shop and retailers connect with the customers. These channels include in-store, online, catalog, call center, mobile apps, social media, and so forth. Omnichannel is the means by which retailers and consumers engage with each other across touchpoints through one seamless customer experience. There is truly a plethora of touchpoints, including in-store, website, mobile site, mobile apps, Snapchat, Twitter, Pinterest, Instagram, Facebook, YouTube, and Amazon. The digital landscape also describes the mix of channels.

Due to the increase in channels, retailers are adjusting their business processes and technology to support omnichannel initiatives. Some retailers have separate buying teams for e-commerce versus in-store. In general, retailers are moving away from having separate buying teams to enhance the seamless transition between the channels. If two people are buying for swimwear, for example, it becomes much more difficult to have a cohesive message between in-store and online.

The increase in omnichannel shopping brings its own challenges for retailers. As e-commerce sales continue to grow, store volume declines. We call physical store locations "brick and mortar." Controlling inventory is one of the top challenges. Declining volume in brick-and-mortar locations results in less of a need for inventory to maintain productivity and profitability.

However, studies have shown that customers still enjoy shopping in these locations. They may walk through a store and then purchase via their mobile phone a couple hours later. This behavior is called showrooming. Showrooming brings large complexities to retailers. Maintaining inventory levels as well as staffing to support an increase in traffic but a decline in sales is a challenge. As e-commerce sales started to increase, retailers invested in fulfillment centers, large distribution centers that fulfill online, catalog, and call center orders.

In the last couple of years, since the rise of showrooming, retailers are transitioning to in-store fulfillment. In-store fulfillment supports presentations for customers walking through the stores and supports the staffing for these brick-and-mortar locations. Of course, there are still challenges with this type of approach. Mainly, shipping costs can become a large burden as multiple items in a customer's order may come from different locations. In-store fulfillment from multiple store locations can also have a negative impact on customer experience because the customer is getting 20 boxes in the mail, all at different times. For example, the customer's top may come from store 1, the skirt may come from store 2, and the associated accessories may come from store 3. This creates additional shipping fees for the retailer because the customer only paid one shipping fee, but the retailer had to ship three separate boxes.

To solve this problem, optimization has become a critical piece in the equation. Typically, legacy fulfillment mechanisms were driven by business rules. Business rules are a lot of "if . . . then" statements. Optimization, however, is the selection of the best available scenario, which takes into account multiple factors. In this example, these factors may be the locations that have the largest amount of items in the purchase order, the geographic distance to the shipping address, the amount of inventory of each item within the order, and the like.

An additional challenge that has arisen since the explosion of e-commerce and mobile is the competition. Customers have information at their fingertips. They can find any and all information, including competitor product availability, competitor pricing, and even coupons! Let's face it, who hasn't Googled or looked on Amazon before making a large purchase? Customers are able to check pricing in the middle of retail locations. There is even a "shopping" filter on Google. Couponing has become a hobby in recent years along with thousands of coupon sites and apps. In order to stay in the game, competitor pricing is a key element when thinking about pricing strategies for digital channels.

The third challenge with the rise in e-commerce and the digital landscape is marketing and personalization. E-mail has been flooded in recent years with offers upon offers. Whether it's a percentage off, extra off on clearance, or free shipping, inboxes are being flooded with offers, relevant or not. Offers via apps are also a key strategy. But all of these interaction points with the customer add more complexity to the marketing efforts. We discuss the topic of pricing and marketing efforts in more detail in Chapters 5 and 6.

With these added complexities come large amounts of data. Retail data can be sales, product inventory, e-mail offers, customer information, competitor pricing, product descriptions, social media, and much more. Combined, this is described as big data, or large sets of data that are leveraged to make better business decisions. There has been a lot of buzz and hype about the term "big data" in the last couple of years.

Big data can be described in two ways: structured data and unstructured data. Different types of data can support different initiatives within retail.

In order to leverage the insights gained through analytics successfully, structured versus unstructured data in retail is a key topic to understand. Structured data is data that sits in a database, a file, or a spreadsheet. It is generally organized and formatted. In retail, this data can be point-of-sale data, inventory, product hierarchies, and so on. Unstructured data does not have a specific format. It can be customer reviews, tweets, pictures, and even hashtags.

Now that you know what structured versus unstructured data in retail is, let's talk about how to use it. Customer reviews are a great way to understand why a certain product is or isn't working. Word clouds are tools to visualize large amounts of customer reviews. Finding keywords that are used frequently can give insight into product features. For example, if "fits small" is frequently used, then the retailer can be proactive by adding this to the product description or above the size selection. This will reduce customer returns and money lost on shipping fees.

Unstructured data can also be studied for sentiment analysis. This gives insight into whether the customer's response is positive, negative, or neutral. A great example of this is being able to analyze customers' Twitter responses. Let's say you post a tweet with products you are thinking about buying for your spring line, including a sketch of the design along with a descriptive hashtag such as the brand and the item name. Leveraging advanced technologies, the retailer is able to obtain customer responses related to the hashtag from Twitter and analyze the responses for sentiment analysis. This analysis enables retailers to understand customers' responses before the retailer even buys the product. This technique can also be utilized in season and give merchants insight into areas of opportunity or risk so that they can best manage their business.

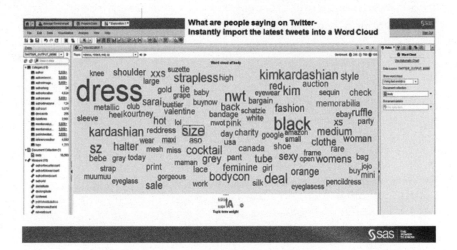

As you can probably tell from reading this chapter, the changing retail environment has made it critical to understand analytics for more detailed analysis of business decisions. Complexities in e-commerce and the digital landscape and new challenges from omnichannel strategies and the world of big data have led to advanced analytics becoming an integral part of retail. In the following chapters, we are going to walk through applications of analytics within the retail environment, including assortment management, pricing decisions, marketing strategies, store operations, and cybersecurity.

CHAPTER **2**

Merchandise Financial Planning

"Assortment" is a term used to describe the product offerings carried by a retailer. Managing this assortment is a critical piece to creating a successful and profitable business. This assortment needs to change with the seasons. It needs to change with the recent fashion trends and consumer trends. Assortments need to reflect what is going on in the marketplace. If people are no longer buying Kodak cameras or overalls, then you definitely don't want them in your assortment. But assortment management is also about having a business plan and meeting financial goals. At the end of the day, no matter how beautiful an assortment is, it has to drive profitability for a retailer or designer to stay in business.

Management of assortment starts at a high level. Specific financial targets must be met. Quite often, these high-level initial targets are determined by a finance department. Companies have certain targets that must be met to keep the lights on, keep investors happy, and make money. Finance departments typically determine a high-level annual revenue target. From there, a planning and allocation team typically takes that number from finance and breaks it down to consumable and actionable levels.

We call these levels hierarchies. A "hierarchy" by definition is a ranking system where items are classified into different levels. From a merchandising hierarchy perspective, three different hierarchies are utilized. One hierarchy is for merchandise, the second hierarchy is location based, and the third is time. People in retail also refer to this as MLT (merchandise, location, and time). The merchandise hierarchy naming and ordering convention can vary by retailer. Typically it starts at the top with "total company." This could then be followed by division or category.

A total company can be divided up into different higher-level businesses. For example, in a department store, these divisions could be: men's, misses', petite, plus/women's, juniors, young men's, boys, girls, baby, shoes, accessories, and home. The next level under a division is typically a department. These departments are lower-level segments of a division. Let's take misses' as an example. Within misses', the lower-level segments of the department could be tops, warm wear, bottoms, dresses, and swim. The next level typically is a major class. Examples of major classes within misses' tops could be long-sleeve tops, short-sleeve tops, and tanks. Some retailers may even take it a next level lower, to subclasses. Below that is the style. Each style of shirt falls under these hierarchical designations, followed by the style in specific colors, which is called a style-color or lot, and then the style-color is organized by size. The lowest level of style-color-size is most often referred to as a SKU, which stands for "stock keeping unit." The SKU often represents the item and has a designated barcode used to track sales and inventory.

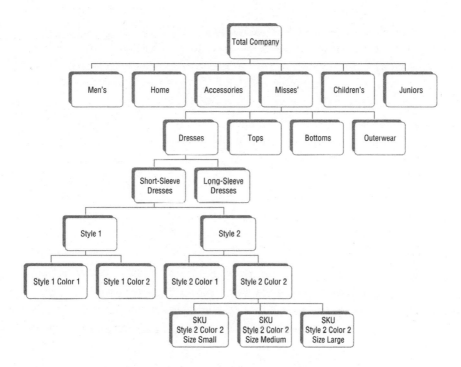

The typical definition of a location hierarchy has changed over the years as e-commerce has grown. Typically, it begins with the total company. If there are different brands, they could follow the total company. Below a brand could possibly be the brick-and-mortar channel and the direct-to-consumer channel, also known as DTC. DTC is another tricky term that can vary widely by retailer. It is the business channel that includes e-commerce. Retailers may also have a wholesale channel of business that sells directly to third-party resellers, such as T.J. Maxx, Ross, department stores, or other outlet stores. Within the location hierarchy, these channels can then be further broken down to lower levels of detail. The brick-and-mortar channel can be broken down by country. Within a country, it can be broken down by region, followed by state and other levels to describe the hierarchy until the lowest level of specific store/location. These stores are assigned a store number along with a store name.

Time has a much more standard hierarchical naming convention. Typically, time starts with a fiscal year. Fiscal is, by definition, an adjective used to describe a noun that is related to government revenue or taxes. The fiscal year of many retailers aligns with the calendar year, starting in January and ending in December. Some retailers, however, have fiscal calendars that do not align with the calendar year. For example, the first fiscal month of the year may be August and the last month is July; or the year may start in February and end in January. The fiscal year can then be broken down into season and/or quarter, followed by month and then week. Very few retailers plan by day, but it could happen. More power to them!

Okay, so now that we have established all of the many different hierarchy levels included in merchandise, location, and time, let's talk about how these are used. As I mentioned earlier, a company's finance department typically determines the highest level of financial targets. Finance is a division within an organization. The planning and allocation team is typically a separate team that is responsible for planning the business at a lower level, tracking performance, reacting to changes, and driving the business forward. This team can also differ in their exact naming convention by retailer, but their roles and responsibilities are typically standard.

Once the planning and allocation team receives the overall financial target, they then create a financial plan at the lower levels of the merchandise, location, and time hierarchy. They do this in order to better understand the business, react to trends, find risks and opportunities, and quickly react or course correct. The merchandise planners create a financial and strategic plan that includes key performance indicators, or KPIs. KPIs are metrics that indicate the performance of the business. These concepts and activities are known as merchandise financial planning.

In merchandise financial planning, typically sales, inventory, margin, and productivity KPIs are planned. Sales KPIs include total sales compared to regular-priced sales, clearance or markdown sales, and e-commerce sales. These sales can also be planned, tracked, and monitored in dollars/currency or units. Inventory KPIs include inventory on hand, inventory that is on its way or planned to be received (also known as on order), and planned receipts, which expresses how much inventory you plan to bring in each quarter, month, or week. One example of a margin KPI is gross margin. Gross margin is the money made or net profit when you take the total dollar sales of an item and/or level of the hierarchy and subtract what it cost for that item. For example, if I sell a long-sleeved top for twenty dollars and I had to pay ten dollars to make or buy that shirt from another source, then the gross margin is ten dollars. The gross margin percent is the percentage of profit earned from sales. For example, we earned ten dollars of gross margin from the shirt that we bought and sold. We bought it for ten dollars and sold it for twenty dollars; ten dollars divided by twenty dollars is a 50 percent gross margin.

$20 Total Sales − $10 Cost of Goods = $10 Gross Margin

$10 Gross Margin / $20 Total Sales = 50% Gross Margin

The hierarchy levels at which these KPIs are planned depend on the retailer. There is almost always a merchandise financial plan at the department level. Referring back to our misses' division example, this would be a merchandise financial plan for tops, warm wear, bottoms, dresses, and swim. This lower-level merchandise financial plan can be broken down to major class or subclass as well. These plans are typically created by merchandise planners to give guidance to their merchant or buyer counterparts to help keep to their budget and fiscal targets.

In addition to sales planning, inventory is a critical component of the planning process because without it, sales just cannot happen. Retailers are investing their money into inventory with the hope of driving sales and demand at a price higher than the cost they paid for it. Timing is crucial. Inventory planning is all about getting the right product in the right stores or channels at the right time. For example, you can't bring jackets to Florida in March and expect to sell any.

When creating a merchandise financial plan, you also have to factor in what you are already carrying into a season before the season starts. There is a natural product life cycle; you must ensure that you are planning inventory throughout the season, increasing for anticipated demand and decreasing for anticipated lows. You must also flow inventory. Flow is a key concept here. Flowing inventory means that you are keeping the assortment fresh and new, not just bringing in all jackets in November and nothing else. Is there a store that you visit frequently? Do you visit to check out the new items in hopes that you may find that cute pair of stilettos you had in mind? Finding new products on your frequent store visits is due to the fact that retailers flow new, fresh inventory into the store throughout the season to attract customers and keep them coming back for more.

As inventory sells down, additional items are needed to fill the stock. Additional items that are ordered but not yet in the store or the distribution center are classified as on order. Typically, a weekly inventory plan is created by the merchandise financial planner. To get to the target inventory plan, merchandise planners determine the projected inventory that they will start the week with and what is on order. On order refers to the inventory that has been purchased by the retailer and accounted for as on its way to the store locations. This inventory has either been shipped or will be shipped at some point to the stores or distribution center. The combination of current inventory, inventory on its way or scheduled to ship during a certain time, and sales is then compared to the inventory merchandise planners would ideally like to have. The difference between what you will have and what you actually need is called receipts. Receipts are units and/or dollar amounts of inventory needed to get back to the ideal inventory necessary to drive profitable sales. These receipts are what the merchant uses to buy the items from vendors. Receipts basically are merchants' open checkbooks.

The four main concepts here:

1. Plan the sales.
2. Determine the optimal inventory levels.
3. Factor in inventory on the way as on order.

Current Inventory + On Order − Sales Plan = Projected Inventory

4. Project how much inventory you need to get to an optimal level as receipts.

$$\text{Optimal Inventory} - \text{Projected Inventory} = \text{Receipts}$$

Merchandise financial plans help capture the higher-level risks and opportunities. These financial plans help guide merchants on their assortment decisions. The merchandise financial planning process is the first step to merchandise assortment management. Assortment management begins with preparing this high-level strategic plan followed by breaking it down by item and then breaking it down again by size.

There is an art to each step of the merchandise assortment management process: merchandise financial planning, assortment planning, size scaling, and pricing. Art in retail is an integral piece of the process. From understanding the key category trends, such as a shift from capris to jeans, to having an eye for those "it" pieces within a collection, merchants are the vision generators. Now let's take a look at how we can leverage analytics to make these processes more accurate and efficient and help retailers achieve a competitive advantage.

STATISTICAL FORECASTING

Merchandise financial planning, as we explained earlier, is the process of planning different financial metrics, such as sales. Statistical forecasting is a key competitive advantage for retailers when planning. Statistical forecasting leverages historical sales to predict future demand. These sales typically have patterns associated with them that can be statistically modeled and forecast with a great degree of accuracy. These patterns are normally related to trend, seasonality, and/or holidays. Other related factors (patterns) also can influence demand (purchases), such as merchandising tactics, markdown pricing, in-store promotions, and events. These influence factors, or what is referred to as causal variables, can also be statistically modeled (sensed) and used to shape (predict) future demand. Historical sales can contain one of these patterns (components), a combination, or even all.

Seasonality, by definition, is a pattern that is predictable. For example, every year during the months of July and August, children's clothing sales peak, due to the back to school season. The back to school season occurs every year; therefore, an increase in sales in the children's department is predictable. If you were to graph the sales over time, you would see a recurring pattern. This is another key benefit of being able to visualize data.

In addition to seasonality, trends are common components of historical data. Trend is a general direction that something is moving in an increasing, decreasing, or steady direction over time. Trends can occur across the product portfolio at multiple levels of the hierarchy. For example, the misses' tops department could be maintaining a steady pattern, but crochet tops are trending up. You can also have a combination of both seasonality and trends.

The third type of historical sales components are in-store promotions, events, and holidays. Promotions and events occur in distinct time periods in history when a specific event occurred that is not a normal occurrence. For example, an event could be the Olympics or the Super Bowl taking place near a retailer's location. Promotions can also run during holiday periods in an attempt to sell more products, get more store traffic, and/or reduce excess on-hand inventory. During these promotions and/or events, sales normally spike for a certain length of time (duration of the promotion or event), and that spike most likely will not occur again in the future unless the retailer initiates another promotion and/or event. Onetime events may also create declines in sales for a certain period of time. An example of this occurred when I was a merchandise planner and the sprinkler system broke in a location and destroyed the store's dress department. Dress sales declined significantly. However, this decline was only temporary until new merchandise arrived. This type of event is known as an outlier; outliers need to be identified and quantified using statistics to adjust the sales history. Holidays also need to be accounted for in the historical data if the holiday shifts or is not tied to a specific date. Black Friday and Mother's Day are great examples of shifting holidays because these holidays do not occur on the same calendar date year over year.

Other causal factors that can impact sales history and can be used to influence (shape) future demand are price changes, sales promotions, coupons, and other external factors that are driven by marketing departments to increase sales traffic. As we mentioned, various outliers in historical demand values need to be identified and used to statistically adjust the sales history. An example would be that the average store sells 20 pairs of girls' cheerleading shorts a week. A cheerleading coach comes into the store and buys 60 pairs for her squad. The sales for that day would fall out of the normal sales pattern and may be considered an outlier. Using statistics, we can identify that outlier and use it to adjust historical demand, so that it doesn't artificially inflate our future forecast and cause excess inventory.

Due to the need to consider seasonality, trends, sales promotions, events, in-store merchandising tactics, outliers, and other related factors, manual sales planning can be an extremely difficult task. Analytics can really help an organization drive accuracy and efficiency here. Now, not all forecasting solutions are created equal. Some solutions have many more capabilities than others. You definitely want to keep this in mind and ask the questions to understand what capabilities each solution can bring to a retailer or brand. Forecasting solutions can be like buying a car. You can buy a Kia that has a CD player and automatic locks or you can buy a Mercedes that has a CD player, Bluetooth, iTunes, a backup camera, DVD player, and, of course, performance.

The strongest forecasting solutions include capabilities to take into account seasonality, trends, sales promotions, in-store merchandising factors, marketing vehicles, events, and outliers. The SAS Institute is a privately held software company that has been in business since 1976. SAS stands for "Statistical Analysis System," which is an analytical software language and suite to support predictive analytics, data management, and business intelligence. The software company also offers analytical software solutions to support business functions across all industries. One of these solutions is statistical forecasting. The best-of-breed forecasting processes, such as SAS Statistical Forecasting, include the following steps:

Step 1: In statistical forecasting, you determine the first step of the process. This usually occurs in a click-through user interface. You determine the forecast horizon, which is the amount of time that you would like to forecast into the future. This most often coincides with the planning calendar. Typically six months to a year out is what is leveraged in merchandise financial planning. You also determine a holdout period. Think of a holdout period as a time in history that has already occurred, and you are setting it to the side for a moment. Once you have completed the first step, the forecasting solution then does the heavy lifting for you.

1 Define holdout period for model selection

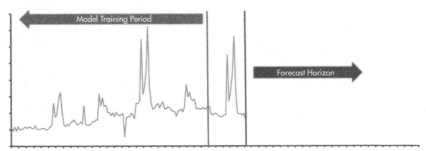

Step 2: The forecasting solution goes through a forecasting process to predict the future demand. The forecasting process analyzes historical sales, also known as training history, to see if there are any patterns associated with sales promotions, in-store merchandising factors, events, and/or outliers. The process determines if these factors were significant, meaning whether they affected sales. If so, these factors are leveraged to shape and predict future demand using "what-if" analysis.

② Diagnose training history

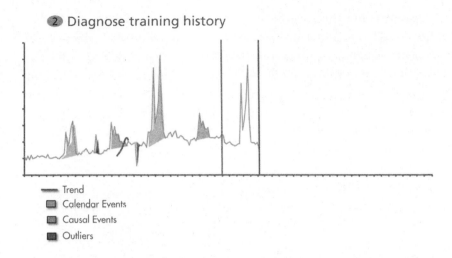

▬▬ Trend
▢ Calendar Events
▢ Causal Events
▣ Outliers

Step 3: Once the historical sales have been analyzed, the forecasting process goes through hundreds of different forecasting models to forecast the holdout period. It's basically going through and saying "Okay, if this sample of history had not yet happened, then how close would I have predicted these sales with the different forecasting models?" Think of these models as different calculations for predicting future demand.

③ Construct competing models

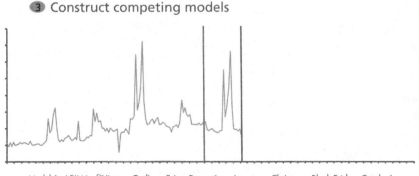

Model 1: ARIMA, *f*(History, Outliers, Price, Promotions, Inventory, Christmas, Black Friday, Catalog)
Model 2: Exponential Smoothing, *f*(History, Seasonality)
Model 3: ARIMA, *f*(History, Outliers, Price, Christmas, Catalog)

Step 4: The forecasting process then compares the predicted sales with the actual sales to calculate how far off the forecast was from the actuals. We call these error measures. Common measures that can be utilized are mean absolute error (MAE), mean absolute percent error (MAPE), or root mean squared error (RMSE). Think of it like this: The MAE is the difference in quantity between the predicted sales and the actual sales. The MAPE tells you how inaccurate the forecast was as a percentage. So if the MAPE is 15%, then the forecast is said to be 85% correct and 15% incorrect.

④ Forecast & evaluate holdout period model performance

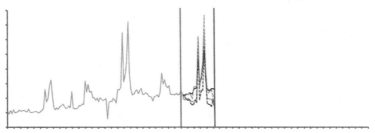

Error	
13.64%	Model 1: ARIMA, f(History, Outliers, Price, Promotions, Inventory, Christmas, Black Friday, Catalog)
11.05%	Model 2: Exponential Smoothing, f(History, Seasonality)
8.58%	Model 3: ARIMA, f(History, Outliers, Price, Christmas, Catalog)

Step 5: The forecasting process selects the forecasting model with the lowest error for the series.

⑤ Select champion model and refit over entire history

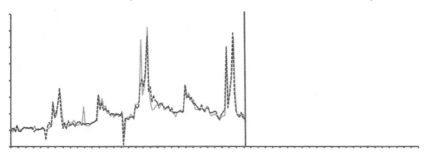

Model 3: ARIMA, f(History, Outliers, Price, Christmas, Catalog)

Step 6: The forecasting process takes the winning forecasting model, then leverages all of the historical data, including the holdout period, and forecasts the future demand. Forecasting analysts also have the ability to run "what if" or scenario analysis by varying the values of those causal factors to proactively shape future demand. For example, if we raise the price by 10% on women's fashion jeans, or run another 10% off sales promotion, how will that impact future demand? In Chapter 5 we discuss how leveraging advanced analytical pricing solutions can automate this type of scenario analysis to recommend what the best approach for the business should be.

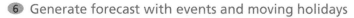

6 Generate forecast with events and moving holidays

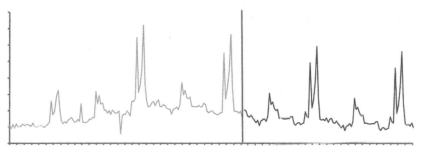

Statistical forecasting helps retailers predict future sales more accurately by accounting for the different components of data and factors that influence demand. Having a more accurate sales plan that takes all of these factors into account enables retailers to make better business decisions. Earlier we mentioned that merchandise planners also plan inventory. But the inventory retailers carry within their channels needs to be in line with their sales demand. If it's not and demand was planned too high, then retailers end up with too much or leftover inventory at the end of the season. This inventory then becomes clearance. If retailers sell inventory at a clearance price, they are not making as much profit. If demand was planned too low, then retailers may run out of inventory and therefore miss sales. This is often referred to as a missed opportunity. It is critical to find that sweet spot and plan sales accurately.

Statistical forecasting also brings efficiency to the process because a forecasting engine does the heavy lifting, allowing merchandise planners to generate more forecasts in a shorter time than through a manual process. Increased accuracy and efficiency of the planning process also enables merchandise planners to focus their time on other core initiatives within the company and continue to help drive the business forward. Retailers are also able to reforecast, taking into account the most recent history and trends. Planners can react much more quickly and proactively adjust for the future on an exception basis rather than manually adjusting (touching) every product every forecast cycle. In addition to increasing accuracy and efficiency in sales planning, statistical forecasting also aids in the planning of inventory.

CHAPTER **3**

Assortment
Management

Historically, merchants have been product centric. "Product centric" means they have been focused on what products they carry and bring to the market. Fashion trends can change from season to season. Customer preferences are ever-evolving. The channels or mechanisms by which customers are shopping or buying are rapidly changing. Customer choices are at an all-time high, and competition is at the customers' fingertips. Many retailers maintain a standardized assortment among their locations. Other retailers vary their assortment among locations as well as channels, such as e-commerce. Retailers are beginning to find that in order to stay in the game, they have to move from being product centric to *customer* centric. How do retailers best vary the product offerings to increase customer satisfaction? How do retailers tailor the assortment to target specific customers walking into each and every location?

In the beginning of my retail planning/merchandising career, I started out in the juniors division of a corporate office. I was so excited to be in a division where I could wear the clothes that I worked with. I thought, This is the coolest job! Picking out cute clothes all day is what I was meant to do! A year or so later, I moved to the misses' sportswear division. I thought to myself, No worries, cute clothes are easy to pick out in any area. Well, I thought wrong.

You see, I was working at a retailer in Florida and in the conservative misses' area. After I attended my first hit-or-miss meeting, I had a wake-up call. During hit-or-miss meetings, merchants display their top items that exceeded their sales plans and the bottom items that didn't. I thought it was a joke at first. . . . The very first hit was far from a hit in my book. I thought, There is no way there are roughly 3,200 women walking around wearing that bedazzled hot pink shirt with flamingoes and seagulls swallowing up the fabric or those purple pants with an elastic waist. Then there was a very cute peasant top that I would wear and I thought, "Okay, good, at least you would have picked out one of the hits." Sure enough, it was a miss! I suddenly had a metallic taste in my mouth and thought, OMG, I am going to be horrible in this area.

Merchandising is not as easy as you may think. It's about selecting merchandise for different groups of individuals who may not all have the same taste as you. So how do we go about figuring out what to buy? This is an age-old question. . . . There's competitive shopping, but by this time you are already behind the trend. The largest tactic for conquering this question has been analyzing what sold in the past. Many merchants try to bring items back in the next season that had mediocre performance the previous season only to then find that they are this season's dogs. Customers are constantly changing and evolving. Do you buy items that you already have? No, of course not. So then how do you determine what customers will want? That is the magic question to assortment planning that we can leverage analytics to answer.

UNDERSTANDING YOUR CUSTOMER

Assortment planning is planning out the item selection within the constraints of the merchandise financial plan. We discussed in Chapter 2 the concept of inventory and merchandise receipts. Merchants/buyers are tasked with spending these receipts with a goal of selecting the best assortment to attract customers and drive sales. The first step in this process is understanding who your customers are and what their preferences are. If a retailer had varying assortments within its stores, then historically these assortments were created for clusters of locations. Store clustering is the grouping of retail stores based on similarities. This clustering made planning how much you need to buy more manageable. A location cluster is a group of locations. Typically these clusters are created in two ways. The first way is by volume grade. Location sales are used to determine the top volume, or "A" volume, locations. These are the top performers with the highest sales. The A volume cluster is followed by B, C, D, and so forth clusters, depending on how many ranks retailers wanted to manage and how much their volume varied.

This is also where sales indices come into play. A sales index is merely a comparison to the average. Sales indices can also be created for different levels of the merchandise and time hierarchy, such as annual, seasonal, monthly, or weekly. We take historical sales from all locations or channels and calculate an average. From there, each location is compared to the average. Let's say an average store sells $1,000 in the misses' tops department a week. Store 1 sells $3,500 a week in the misses' tops department. We simply divide $3,500 by $1,000, and Store 1's sales index is 3.5. Therefore, Store 1 does 3.5 times the amount of the average store in volume. Store 2 sells only $500 a week in the misses' tops department. We then divide $500 by $1,000 to calculate an index of 0.5, or half the volume of an average store, and so forth.

The second mechanism for clustering is based on a location attribute. An attribute is basically defined as a characteristic of a hierarchical level. Attributes are used to describe levels of the merchandise and location hierarchy. Attributes are extremely beneficial in analytics so we will talk about them quite frequently when discussing assortment planning. A typical location attribute used in clustering is climate. Stores are clustered based on cold, warm, tropical, and so on. This type of clustering enables merchants to plan different assortments based on the area's climate conditions, preventing locations in New York from having the same assortments as locations in Florida during January. New York is covered in snow then, and people are bundling up. In Florida, people are visiting the beach and enjoying the little time they have with temperatures below 90 degrees.

Clustering can also be done using both climate and volume so that one has their A, B, C, and D volume cold stores and A to D volume warm stores. This type of clustering has been done for years and years. But as the retail landscape evolves to include so many different ways that customers can shop assortments and as competition increases, this concept just isn't cutting it anymore. Retailers face a typical challenge: Two locations can be within minutes of each other, in the same climate and with the same volume. However, they have a completely different customer base with different preferences.

One location may be in an area with a higher average income. Luxury brands and higher price points may sell better here than lower-quality brands or lower price points. The second location does the same volume but is located in a neighborhood of middle-class families that lean more toward lower price points and more affordable brands. If you knew this, would you give them the same assortment? Absolutely not. But when you have 1,000-plus stores, there is no way that buyers could go through and analyze customer preferences for all locations and ensure they are buying the right assortment for each store. These characteristics are also referred to as trade area characteristics. A trade area is the geographic area surrounding a store location. If you were to look at a map of where a store is located, the surrounding area is typically where the majority of the customers reside. Trade area characteristics, such as the average income of the surrounding population, are available. Companies collect this data and then sell it to retailers. This is known as a third-party data source.

TYPES OF CUSTOMER SEGMENTS

NPV PER CUSTOMER

CONVENIENCE SEEKERS

- VALUE CONVENIENCE IN DELIVERY, ORDERING
- HIGH INCOME
- LONG RELATIONSHIP, LARGE REFERRALS

BRAND BUYERS

- BRAND BUYERS, NOT PRICE SENSITIVE
- HIGHEST INCOME. MORE OFTEN MALE
- EXPENSIVE TO ACQUIRE BUT BUY MOST INITIALLY AND REFER MORE

CASUAL BUYERS

- NOT CONCERNED WITH PERISHABLES OR DELIVERY TIME WINDOWS
- SMALL SPENDING GROWTH

RELATIONSHIP SEEKERS

- INFLUENCED BY RETAILER BRAND, SUGGESTIONS, AND PROMOTIONS
- LOW INCOME
- SMALL SPENDING GROWTH/REFERRAL

BARGAIN HUNTERS

- PRICE IS PRIMARY AND PERISHABLES ARE NOT IMPORTANT
- LOW INCOME
- SMALL PURCHASES

SOURCE: BAIN/MAINSPRING ONLINE RETAILING SURVEY

Another challenge when determining customer preferences is the fact that customers shop at multiple retail touchpoints, such as instore, website, apps, and even social media. They also may not shop at their local store and instead travel to another store within their trade area because they may like that mall better. Therefore, you cannot get a true view of customers who are shopping and what their preferences are by grouping together stores based on volume and rank.

In addition to determining how best to assort by location, it has been a struggle to understand and plan different channels, such as in-store versus e-commerce, because the data may have not supported an omnichannel process. Sales data may have been stored only to reflect the total sales, not breaking it out by channel.

The lack of data visibility broken out by channel has begun to change in recent years and will continue to evolve as the digital landscape evolves. Retailers are moving toward separating point-of-sale data to support the process. Marketing departments typically have access to sales data by customer. This data is rich in insights, but it has been restricted only to marketing. Marketers were responsible for customers, and merchants were responsible for stores. But this is changing.

This data should be leveraged in the assortment planning process to get a true omnichannel vision of customer preferences and demand across all channels. Having a true picture of customer preferences by demand zone area will give buyers a true 360-degree vision of demand. This is where data management comes into play. "Data management" is a term that describes the act of managing different data sources and data types to standardize in order to leverage for analytics. Analytics are only as good as the data.

Customer-level data typically has an associated zip code. Have you ever been to the store and been asked for your zip code at the register? This information is stored for marketing efforts, but the future of retail will involve leveraging such data for other uses, such as assortment planning. Using data management techniques, retailers can determine which brick-and-mortar location is closest to a customer's zip code and associate sales with that specific trade area. Retailers can then combine sales data from in-store and online sales from their shoppers to get a full view of their customers. From there, buyers would be able to see what customers in that area are buying in-store and online. They may be buying certain items online because they aren't carried in the store. This holistic picture of customers across channels can help retailers understand how best to assort by channel and what fulfillment strategies work best.

This omnichannel view of the customer aids in localization efforts. Localization is the act of creating merchandise assortments specific to local markets. The term is used to describe the act of localizing stores and leveraging store-specific data. The challenge is that localizing is a much more detailed activity than assorting the historical way by volume and/or climate. This is where analytics comes into play. Analytics can aid buyers' localization efforts by providing a lower level of clustering as well as leveraging rich customer data efficiently.

"Data mining" is a term used to describe analyzing large amounts of data to find patterns, correlations, and similarities. Data mining techniques can be leveraged to cluster locations as well as similar trade areas. This technique can also be leveraged to cluster specific customers for marketing efforts, as we discuss in Chapter 6. Data mining to look at similar selling patterns of style-colors or items to cluster trade areas is a much more intelligent approach to clustering than the traditional approach of looking just at in-store data and clustering locations based on volume or climate. Clustering trade areas looking at all channel demand based on similar customer preferences moves retailers from product centric to becoming more customer centric. These similar style-colors, or items, can then be analyzed by merchandise attributes. Merchandise attributes are characteristics that describe the merchandise, such as color, sleeve length, fabric type, silhouette, and many more. These location clusters can also be joined together with demographic information as well as location attributes. This gives a true profile of average customers who are walking into each and every one of your locations, what they are buying, how they are buying, and where there is opportunity to effectively localize assortments.

Each cluster then has information about the market, such as average age, average income, marital status, and education levels. This information can be leveraged to understand whether there is, let's say, a large number of millennials in the area. Should we bring in more brands targeted at this age group? Is the location in a retirement market? These two customers are looking for very different assortments; therefore, localization efforts are easily identified. The customer becomes the center of the product selection.

UNDERSTANDING PRODUCT CHOICE COUNTS

The next step in the assortment planning process is understanding how many products should go into each cluster of stores and how much of each product. The array of merchandise choices is referred to as breadth. You can't create a dress department with just two styles and expect to do business. No one wants to be the girl or guy in the same outfit as someone else at the party. Even worse is losing the contest of "who wore it best?" The next concept is depth. Depth is the amount of each style-color you carry on the floor. Six units of that perfect new Michael Kors little black dress may just not be enough.

I'll never forget my days of working at Forever 21, a high-fashion retailer with low price points aimed at the younger market. On a Saturday morning, we would put out 24 units of some style-colors, and they would be completely gone by lunch. Determining the right amount of breadth and depth of the assortment is critical to ensuring you are not missing an opportunity or flooding a store with too much inventory.

Analytics can aid in this decision-making process. The first type of analytic that can be leveraged as a component is a statistical forecast. We described the forecasting process in detail in regard to planning merchandise sales demand. The statistical forecast can also be generated at a location level. Understanding the future demand of each location, taking into account seasonality, trends, and causal factors such as promotions, events, and outliers, can help determine how much breadth and depth is needed.

Other factors that may be taken into account when determining the breadth and depth is case packs or prepacks. When merchandise is bought from a vendor or designer, it might come in a predefined pack. For example, I may buy basic white T-shirts from a vendor, and the shirts come in prepacks or case packs of six units. The pack of six units contains one unit that is size small, two units that are size medium, two units that are size large, and one unit that is size extra-large. The pack arrives in a plastic-wrapped package containing the six units. I could order as many of these packs as I need, but the quantity must be divisible by the multiple of the pack, which in this case is six. For example, I can order 300 units and I would get 50 six-piece case packs. But I couldn't order 305 because it is not a multiple of six.

Other vendors may offer product only in bulk. "Bulk" is a term that describes product that comes in multiples of ones. Think of a massive box with all 305 T-shirts that I would like to order. This gives merchants more flexibility on what and how much is bought, but it can also cause inefficiencies in the supply chain. We discuss these inefficiencies later in Chapter 4.

Merchants may also have to account for vendor minimums. "Vendor minimum" is a term that describes a minimum buy quantity that merchants must meet in order to purchase the product. A vendor minimum ensures that the vendor is meeting its productivity goals. Vendors do not want to go through the effort of buying materials for their factories to make two shirts. That's just not practical. The more vendors can save on materials by making mass quantities and efficiently running their factories, the lower their costs can be. The lower their costs, the more profit retailers can make on the merchandise.

In addition to forecasted sales, vendor constraints such as case packs, and vendor minimums, there is still the art to the science of determining the optimal breadth and depth of assortments. Merchants may have specific presentation minimums to support the artistic visual merchandising element. For example, merchants do not want to walk into their smallest store and see fewer than six pieces of a product. If it's two pieces of something, it may get lost in a sea of merchandise. Instead of a beautiful-looking floor of product, it will look like a garage sale. Merchants may also never want to see any more than a certain amount. For example, a merchant might not want to walk into a store and see more than 48 pieces of a certain item. An average fixture holds about 96 units at a minimum, so seeing half a fixture of one item is not attractive to customers. It goes back to the concept of no one wanting to show up to the party in the same outfit as someone else. It also hurts the sense of urgency. Customers may be indecisive about buying something. I know I am the most indecisive person ever when it comes to shopping. If there is too much depth, customers may think that it will still be there later if they decide they really want it. If there are fewer items, they may think they should just go ahead and buy it so they don't miss out. Of course, these presentation standards are very dependent on the retailer's overall strategy and vision. For example, discount stores, such as outlet stores, may strategically plan a smaller depth of assortments, such as two items of a product. They create a "treasure hunt" type of shopping experience. Some customers love this concept and feel like they struck gold when they find a cute top at an affordable price and in their size. Department stores have presentation standards to prevent customers from having to hunt. They execute very inviting visual presentations. Boutiques may have a mixture of both concepts. A retailer's assortment breadth and depth strategy also depends on the product and the rate of sale. If it is a jewelry department that may sell one of the items every other month, then clearly the buyer is going to plan for less depth.

How can buyers take into account the forecasted sales by store within their clusters, vendor constraints, their vision, and the art? Analytics! "Optimization" is a term used to describe analytics that calculate and determine the most ideal scenario. Optimization procedures analyze each scenario and supply a score. An optimization analytic can run through hundreds, even thousands of scenarios, and rank each one based on a target that is being achieved. Therefore, buyers can leverage optimization to determine the most ideal breadth and depth of their assortment, taking these factors into account along with the statistical forecasted sales.

UNDERSTANDING CURRENT PRODUCT PERFORMANCE

Once we understand who the customers are that we are targeting and how much each cluster of stores needs from a depth and breadth perspective, the next step in the process is understanding what is really driving the business. This type of analysis can be done before a season starts as buyers are planning out their next season and analyzing the past season. Understanding what items are really driving the business is a key task in understanding how to move forward. This type of insight can direct you to what items you may want to keep in your assortment and bring to the next season. We often refer to this concept as product rationalization. Product rationalization will also give insight into what items are not working and you should consider dropping from the season. It can also give insight into what kinds of items are your top performers if it's a fashion area where the assortment is changing season over season.

This step in the process can also be a very emotional one. It's extremely hard for anyone to admit defeat. Who wants to admit that they bought a dog? You become emotionally attached to the product and keep trying to give it another shot. It's like a bad relationship. You tell yourself, It will pick up eventually; just give it another week.

Traditionally, this type of activity and performance review was thought of as reporting. Information technology typically would provide some type of reporting mechanism. This reporting could be through an Excel spreadsheet process, a reporting solution, or even green bar reports. Green bar reports are typically 14 7/8" wide with perforated edges. Every other line is green to help the reader follow the data on the large reports. The earlier editions of green bar reports had four lines green and then four lines white. The pages of this report were fan folded. This type of reporting paper made its debut in the 1970s. Some of you may have never even seen a green bar report. These are definitely old school, but people are still using them today. Once buyers have the performance report, the data historically is analyzed manually. It could be anywhere from highlighting the green bar report to sorting and conditional formatting in Excel.

When I first started out in retail, I used green bar reports. The reports were printed by going to a series of black and green font screens to execute. Once the year was over and a new year started to log actual sales, the report was no longer available. Therefore, if you didn't print it out, you had no visibility into historical performance. Even worse, if you printed out the report but accidentally threw it away, spilled coffee on it, or took over a new area and couldn't find it, you were just out of luck. Hard to believe that I am referring to 2012 here. Although this company has since moved leap years into the future, companies that haven't been able to modernize still rely on this green bar method.

Once you had the data, it was a manual process to analyze, with added emotional decision making, as discussed earlier. The manual assortment insights were a consideration when creating the assortment. Most often, it was not connected or integrated. Not only is this not efficient, but there is also a large degree of error.

This is where analytics come into play. Analytics can be applied to previous historical performance or future statistical forecast values to understand where there is risk and opportunity. Analytics can automate this process and analyze Big Data more accurately and efficiently than the human eye can. Analytics can also enable users to analyze additional elements that may not otherwise be considered due to the scope of elements and items that would need to be reviewed. Manually analyzing an entire assortment of a category could take weeks. An analytical process can reduce that time period to less than a minute. An example of this process would be to analyze an entire assortment, looking at sales performance, gross margin, and inventory productivity, and other factors to populate recommendations on what items should be kept in the assortment and what should be dropped. This method also gives insight into how you can make big bigger!

Demand transference is another area when looking at an assortment. "Demand transference" is the understanding of how demand can cross over between similar or correlated categories. For example, if I remove all of the camisoles in the assortment, how will that affect the sales of sheer items? Understanding how removing items from an assortment may affect other items that you are keeping in the assortment is important.

Another factor that can be taken in to account when analyzing and rationalizing an assortment is cannibalism. "Cannibalism" in assortment planning decisions is the concept that some items may hurt the sale of other items and eat up a portion of their demand. Let's take brands as an example. Some retailers have their own brand in addition to carrying other brands in their stores. Their own brand is referred to as a private brand or "private label." This brand is found only at that retailer, nowhere else. Private brands can also have lower price points. Since it's their own brand, retailers typically use lower price points to drive interest and compete with national brands.

Active clothing has really started to trend higher over the last couple of years. With the rise in Lululemon and more millennials leading the force to a "clean eating, fit life," retailers are also riding the wave with active clothing brands such as Nike, Champion, and Under Armour. However, Nike and Under Armour brands are high price points and have restrictions on being able to promote them. Retailers have created their own private label active brands to complement the assortment. If it is a new item or private label line, for example, retailers may need to take into account how much these new private label items will cannibalize the sales of other brands. They need to take this into account because it will change the projected demand and therefore demand and inventory must be adjusted in the items sales plan. If not, buyers could buy too much and end up with excess inventory.

An additional data point that must be leveraged in understanding product performance is unstructured data. We briefly touched on concepts of applications of unstructured data in Chapter 1. Unstructured data, such as text from social media, customer reviews, and ratings, is not commonly used today in product rationalizing but is the way of the future.

Being able to leverage all of the rich data of opinions that are out there in the social media world of a retailer's customers is an untapped gold mine. Some are slowly starting to experiment with this concept— as the Kardashians, a family of models and reality television stars, are doing. They have a strong social media presence and also make their audience feel like they are a part of their personal life and business. They have posted items on their Twitter pages and asked their followers which color they liked better. With the latest technology in unstructured data, we can operationalize this concept into the assortment management process.

Text mining is the ability to analyze large amounts of unstructured text data. We can group together words that are most often used together or that are correlated. We can also analyze responses through sentiment analysis. "Sentiment," by definition, is an emotion or feeling. We can analyze the emotion of text to determine whether it is a negative response, a positive response, or neutral. This analysis enables buyers to understand what the response is to the new black dress that they just posted on Twitter.

Was the sentiment negative, positive, or neutral? If the response rate is high, then you would definitely want this information in your assortment planning process so that you could identify where you may need to order more. Or if an item has a negative response, then buyers would be able to quickly react to cancel units on order or work with their vendor to replace the order with different items. When buyers buy products, they may buy an amount following the initial order to fill stores back in that sold out. This is known as a reorder. However, if an item is not selling well, chances are, buyers will want to negotiate with the vendor to cancel the items on order and buy something else.

This sentiment factor can also be a numerical factor that can be used in analytical product rationalization. Think about retailers that are now posting pictures of their assortment on Instagram. Leveraging the amount of likes compared to other products is another way to utilize social media data. Star ratings on websites is a third way. These social touchpoints will become a key component to assortment planning in the future. Test and measure is an activity that retailers have used for years to test what products would perform well in certain areas or markets. These new products may be new brands or even certain trends. Traditionally, retailers would select a group of stores with varying volume, climate, and demographics to measure the performance. Based upon the performance in each market, the new products would then be expanded to stores in the successful markets. Sometimes this test and measure approach ended in excess inventory in markets that did not perform and hurt profit margins. Now retailers are able to leverage social media as a test and measure component to understand which customers like their products on Instagram. Retailers are leveraging sentiment analysis to understand the customers' emotional responses to their products and then using this information to assort new products to ideal markets.

"Key influencers" is another method of assortment planning that will evolve over the next couple of years to become the norm. With the rise in social media such as Pinterest and Instagram, fashion bloggers have increased in number. A fashion blogger is an individual who either has a website or social media profile dedicated to modeling and writing about the latest hot trends. Some of these individuals have large followings and strongly influence their followers. Some bloggers have millions of followers. We can utilize these individuals to gain a read on future performance. If bloggers are including a certain type of style or item in their blogs or highlighting this item in their social media accounts, retailers can leverage these data elements to predict how well the item will perform. Bloomingdale's, Harrods, and Bergdorf Goodman are some retailers that have begun leading the market in leveraging fashion bloggers to promote their brands and create buzz.

In 2016, retailers began realizing the value of this data and have leveraged the insights through reporting. In the future, retailers must actually take this information and operationalize it into their workflow process for it to be truly meaningful.

As you can imagine, analyzing an entire assortment seems impossible with so many data elements, historical or forecasted sales, KPIs, demand transference, cannibalism, sentiment analysis, Instagram likes, and customer ratings. Analytics can give retailers the ability to operationalize these elements into analytical insights that drive assortment decisions. Each element becomes incredibly impactful to managing assortments throughout the life cycle and season to determine what is truly driving the business and where there is risk and opportunity. Multiple data elements can be used in an analytical process known as an algorithm. An "algorithm" is a series of steps or calculations used to solve a problem. In this example, the data elements can be calculated in a series to determine the optimal action. These actions can include keeping or dropping the product by channel, cluster of stores or trade areas, or locations. This type of automated, analytical approach to rationalizing an assortment leads to localized, customer-centric assortments to drive profitability and efficiency for the retailer.

PREDICTING THE EVOLUTION OF TRENDS

Once retailers have an understanding of who their customers are who are walking into each and every one of their locations, an understanding of the optimal breadth and depth of the assortment, and an understanding of the items that are truly driving the business and what items to drop from the assortment, the next step is to understand what to replace the rest with. What is the evolution of the trends? What is the next hot thing?

Imagine that you are strolling through your favorite department store's dress department. There are so many dresses to choose from, but you also know your own style. You may love maxi dresses or any style of bohemian print dresses. You also notice certain prints like chevron can be seen in all the dress departments where you shop, or crochet fabric. These are examples of merchandise attributes. Merchandise attributes, for example, are color or color family, sleeve lengths, silhouettes, fits, fabric, brand, and many more.

We are now able not only to predict future sales using a statistical forecast, we can also predict future fashion trends by analyzing merchandise attributes. Of course, fashion trends also require a sense of art along with how the market is shaping trends. However, leveraging analytics can give insight into possible items that were never in the assortment that would perform well. Merchandise attributing varies dramatically by retailer. Some retailers have a very mature merchandise attributing process where the merchandise attributes are assigned as items are initially loaded into their core systems. Retailers may have standard merchandise attributes to choose from. Some retailers have a merchandise attributing process, but it is not standardized. It is more done by user, not required, and there may not be data standards. Other retailers may not have any process at all. But merchandise attributing is a business process that every retailer is moving toward because the value is clear.

The merchandise attributes that are analyzed by retailers can also range in number. More attributes are not always better. Analyzing too many attributes can become overwhelming, and, quite frankly, the juice may not be worth the squeeze. Correlation analysis can be leveraged to understand which merchandise attributes are correlated. This can help narrow down the number of attributes to a size that can be managed.

Let's use the example of price point and brand. Envision the women's shoe department in an upscale department store. Each designer, including Christian Louboutin, Jimmy Choo, Manolo Blahnik, Tory Burch, Stuart Weitzman, Jessica Simpson, and Steve Madden, is beautifully merchandised on glass tables. Price points can also be assigned to merchandise or grouped into "good," "better," and "best." These designers are frequently correlated with their price grouping. So when you think of Christian Louboutin, the merchandise is typically in the best category, and so forth. Therefore, brand and price grouping in this example are strongly correlated. Instead of spending time analyzing the price grouping and the brand, it makes more sense to analyze the brands.

But what draws customers into the department and what drives their purchasing decisions may also be specific attributes. I know I always head toward the Jessica Simpson heel display because I know the price point is right, the styles are cute, and the shoes are actually comfortable. Unfortunately, I cannot wear heels that are not comfortable, as cute as they might be. I end up looking like a baby deer trying to walk in high, uncomfortable heels. It's not a good look. Now, I know that brand is what is driving my purchasing decisions for heels, but what about every other customer?

There is actually a way to use analytics to statistically determine what merchandise attributes are the most important to customers and then, within those attributes, the specific values of those attributes that have opportunity. We can understand, for example, that brand or fit drives customers' decisions and then, within that, which brands or fits have the most opportunity by cluster. This can be done leveraging regression analysis.

Regression analysis is a statistical modeling process that estimates variable relationships and helps investigate the effects of certain factors on a target. There are multiple types of regression analysis. In this case, the process is helping to understand the importance of attributes to the target, which is sales. We are then able to estimate the importance of each attribute to a customer's purchasing decision and display the results as a percentage.

Regression analysis can also score each individual attribute value at the store cluster level. This gives merchants insight into what colors, brands, fits, silhouettes, and so forth are driving the business in each cluster, helping them to create the assortment plan and localize the assortment. For example, clusters 1 and 3 might be driving the business in high-end brands, such as Christian Louboutin, because the locations have a higher income demographic. But higher heel inches are driving the business in cluster 1, and lower heels or flats are driving the business in cluster 3. Using analytics to determine the best assortment by cluster helps to give insights into decisions that may have been missed if you are trying to manually analyze all of this information. End business users can review the outputs of this type of analysis on pie charts, bar graphs, and other visual objects rather than looking at the raw statistics.

However, what if a cluster of locations never had Christian Louboutin flats? This is where the predictive analytics come into play. Based on how well specific attributes performed in the clusters, we can predict which attribute combinations would have performed well in stores that never carried those assortments. This analysis answers the age-old question, "What should we have carried?" Based on how well the cluster of locations sold flats in general, the color cream, and the brand Christian Louboutin, then we can predict that they will sell a cream Christian Louboutin flat well. These types of predicted values are merchants and buyers dream shopping lists. Of course, there is still a need to blend together the art and the analytics. The strongest color last season could have been plum so the analytics may suggest a plum Christian Louboutin flat. However, the buyer knows that plum was the pop color of fall last year, and this year it is going to be hunter green. So the results could be interpreted as a fashion color Christian Louboutin flat. Buyers' artistry and eye for taste are still integral parts of the assortment curation process. Not only does the use of analytics help serve up these insights efficiently, it can also help drive the business forward and give retailers that competitive advantage they need to stay in the game.

Key influencers can be leveraged to predict which types of merchandise attribute combinations will be the next evolution of fashion as well. Just as we mentioned leveraging fashion bloggers to determine specific item performance, we can also leverage these influencers to look at future performance at a higher-level attribute perspective. Understanding what attributes of products these fashion bloggers are pinning on their Pinterest boards or which items they are featuring on their Instagram accounts is a concept that is definitely evolving. H&M has started to leverage these fashion bloggers to influence design decisions by partnering with Bloglovin, a fashion blog site, to create a mentorship opportunity. These millennials know how to leverage social media to connect and influence individuals, and they are utilizing this platform to accelerate their fashion careers.

Analyzing merchandise attribute performance as well as the influence of fashion bloggers helps retailers determine what products to buy and aids in design decisions and product development. Whether it is leveraging these insights for a retailer's private brand or for a fashion designer's line, this type of analytical approach is becoming key to assortment planning. Certain e-commerce retailers have adopted this approach for customer-level assortments. There is a rising trend of e-commerce retailers that create "styled" customer-level assortments, such as Stitch Fix. Customers sign up and pay a small styling fee. The stylist then selects outfits for the customers, and it is delivered to their doors.

If customers like an item product, they keep it, and Stitch Fix charges their credit card on file and the styling fee paid is applied to the purchase as a credit. If customers don't like an item, they ship it back in a preaddressed shipping package. Each time customers decide yea or nay for an item, Stitch Fix leverages this data to start to learn what the customers like and uses this information for future shipments. Stitch Fix does this by utilizing the merchandise attributes of the items the customers select. Each shipment becomes more and more aligned to customers' taste, and they don't even have to leave the house! The company basically is using analytics to create customer-level, personalized assortments. It's genius!

I actually tested out this concept and signed up for Stitch Fix. I don't know about you, but I love getting mail that isn't a bill! I was so excited for every third Saturday of the month when I got my box of goodies delivered to my doorstep. The first shipment was so-so. By the third and fourth shipment, I was keeping a minimum of three of the five items in the box.

If retailers are going to keep up in the fast-changing market, they have to adopt analytics in to their process. Understanding the evolution of trends and opportunities for items not carried in the assortment helps retailers to determine how to plan the rest of the assortment. This type of analytical approach for line design and assortment planning can also open the doors for adapting additional business models, such as customer-level, personalized assortments.

HOW MUCH TO BUY?

Now that we know who are customer is, how much each cluster of locations needs from a depth and breadth perspective, the items that are driving the business forward, and what to replace the rest of the assortment with, the next step is planning the sales for all of these items. Historically, this was a manual step where buyers had to plan the sales volume themselves. They typically looked at similar items from last year and how much they sold to determine the future sales plans. As you can imagine, this is an inefficient process and can create a lot of inaccuracies. Just as we talked about manually planning sales for a merchandise financial plan at high levels of the hierarchy, the same process goes for determining sales plans for each item.

Just like sales planning for merchandise financial plans, a statistical forecast can be generated at an item level. We face an additional challenge when forecasting down to the item level: historical data. If new items are being selected for an assortment and no historical sales data is associated with these items, it can be a challenge to plan or forecast. This is where we can leverage data management techniques and merchandise attributes. Based on the assigned merchandise attributes of the new items as well as the merchandise description, we can use data management techniques to find similar items that have historical sales and assign the history to the new items. We're able to process big data to generate these similar item assignments.

From there, we can then generate a forward, statistical forecast for the new items. However, there is a second challenge with the historical data when forecasting at such a low level. Some items may have very small sales or have sold very sporadically, also referred to as intermittent demand. It is the law of big numbers. The larger the numbers or historical data, the easier it is to see patterns, trends, and seasonality. In order to ensure we are capturing these components of the data, we use the process of forecast reconciliation. "Forecast reconciliation" is the process of generating a forecast at different levels of the hierarchy and is used to create the final item forecast. The typical reconciliation mechanism for item-level forecasting is called top-down, proportional reconciliation. This process utilizes a forecast at a higher level of the merchandise hierarchy than the item level, such as major class or department. The forecast is then prorated down to the lower levels of the hierarchy based on the percent contribution of the lower-level forecast.

Let's take dresses as an example. If you look at the total dress history, you can more accurately capture trends and seasonality. We can then take the higher dress-level forecast and push it down to the lower style or style-color forecasts based on the lower-level percentage contribution to the higher level. Retailers also leverage key item forecasting to ensure their key business drivers have an appropriate item-level forecast. This reconciliation process can occur at various levels of the merchandise hierarchy as well as the location hierarchy. For example, retailers may forecast their different channels, such as in-store and e-commerce. Retailers may want to forecast demand at the total e-commerce and in-store channel to understand how inventory should be planned for each channel. Within the in-store channel, forecasting at a region or subregion level may help to determine the overall seasonality so reconciliation could be done by subregion and location.

Understanding how much each item in the assortment is going to sell allows buyers to plan an accurate sales plan and the inventory needed to achieve the strategic merchandise financial plan. New item or fashion item sales planning is also a challenge for retailers. When retailers think about new item or fashion item forecasting, there are two components that make up the demand: the demand pattern and the demand volume. Forecasting the pattern of demand to account for trends and seasonality is the first component. Merchandise and location attributes are leveraged in this analysis. We discussed leveraging regression analysis to understand the attributes that are most important to the customer's purchasing decisions to predict trends earlier in the chapter. Regression analysis is the analytical process of statistically quantifying the effect of a variable on a target. It is also a form of machine learning. Machine learning is a type of artificial intelligence that enables computer programs to learn and evolve as additional data is provided. In new item and fashion item forecasting, regression analysis is used to understand the effect of different merchandise attributes in predicting the pattern of demand, and evolves over time as trends and customer preferences change.

Let's walk through an example. Let's say that we are forecasting for a new boy's navy uniform—short sleeve, cotton shirt—and the location is in southwest Florida with a high-income demographic. The regression process analyzes how each of these attributes effects demand patterns. The analysis determines that this shirt's most important attributes when determining the demand pattern are the merchandise attribute of boys, the attribute of uniform, and the location attribute of the South. Because of these attributes, the analytical process looks at other items with historical sales that have these same attributes to determine the forecasted demand pattern. The pattern spikes for the back to school time period between July and August and then levels in September.

The second step of the process is to then leverage regression analysis to understand which merchandise attributes have the strongest impact on predicting demand volume. The analysis determines that this shirt's most important attributes when determining volume are the merchandise attribute of the color being navy, the attribute of uniform, the high-income demographic, and the location attribute of Florida. Because of these attributes, the analytical process looks at other items with historical sales that have these same attributes to determine the forecasted demand volume. If the shirt was a yellow uniform shirt, then the volume may be smaller because navy is a much more common uniform color in Florida schools.

These two components are then added together, taking the demand pattern and the demand volume to determine the new item or fashion item forecast. This process is done in an automated, scalable process, enabling retailers to forecast hundreds or even thousands of new items in an efficient and accurate process.

For new items and previous items, analytics can determine the significance of events and promotions and account for outliers and anomalies in the data. The statistical forecast has been proven to increase accuracy by over 50%.The increase can equate to a significant optimization in inventory, which leads to an increase in gross margin and profitability.

Once you have an accurate prediction of future demand by item, you can plan the inventory needed for the assortment to support future demand and drive profitable sales. One of the hardest tasks with the evolution of omnichannel is understanding how the inventory should be planned by channel. As the e-commerce business continues to grow, it becomes difficult to determine the right amount of inventory in stores and in fulfillment centers. Planning inventory by channel is also a difficult task since showrooming has emerged. In showrooming, customers utilize brick-and-mortar locations as showrooms to see, touch, and feel the product but still purchase via their mobile apps or websites. Therefore, a degree of inventory must be planned for this aspect of the business in certain cases.

Customer-level data is typically stored for marketing activities. This data may contain customers' item-level purchase information, personal information such as age or gender, as well as the method of purchase (in-store or online). Customer-level data can be extremely helpful when determining inventory levels by channel. Determining inventory levels is where we can leverage customer personas. There is the infamous showroomer, who visits the store but most often makes the final purchase via a mobile app. Then there is the diligent researcher, who researches online and in-store for the best deals and leverages price matching. In addition, there is the average mom who makes the majority of her purchases in-store but signs up for all e-mail promotions. Additional personas are determined by analyzing customer-level data. Understanding the average personas within a trade area can give insight into what the best plan for inventory across channels should be. For example, understanding that more than 50 percent of your customer-level data shows true showroomers can support the additional planning of inventory to support presentations.

Once sales and inventory plans are created for the items within the assortment, a reconciliation process is often leveraged. "Reconciliation" is a term that describes the different levels of the hierarchy meeting at intersects and rolling up or matching. A "hard reconciliation" refers to a process in which the item-level assortment plans must roll up or total the sales and inventory plans of the merchandise financial plan targets. A "soft reconciliation" means that the roll-up of these plans can be viewed and validated against the total merchandise financial plan, but the assortment plan and the merchandise financial plan do not necessarily have to equal completely. Instead, the reconciliation can create a collaborative conversation between the merchant and planner to determine the most appropriate action plan.

This process and collaboration ensures that both buyer and planner have one version of the truth and that the strategies at the various levels of the merchandise hierarchy are all working toward a common goal: to create a customer-centric assortment to drive profitability and create a positive customer experience to strengthen customer loyalty.

WHAT SIZES DO I NEED?

Imagine walking through your favorite retail store. You have a job interview coming up for your dream job. You've been working toward this for the last few years. You know you are perfect for this job and you want to look perfect for your interview, whether it's a dapper suit or a gorgeous sheath dress and blazer. You've even got a Pinterest board going with the looks you've been eyeing since you received the e-mail for your first phone interview.

You've got an exact look in mind and you are on a mission. You start in one store, but you just can't seem to find the look so you head to the next. By the third store, you are starting to feel a bit anxious until you turn the corner. Your eyes focus on a mannequin. That is it! You quickly look around for the fixture where these items are hanging. This retailer merchandises items on hangers with the small size rings. Your eyes quickly scan the line and you don't see your size. You hesitate for a moment but then quickly scan the actual tag of the garment to make sure you didn't miss it or find the size on the wrong hanger.

Unfortunately, there was no mistake. The store does not have your size. You feel defeated in a time where you need as much confidence and drive as possible. You also feel frustrated because this isn't the first time it has happened to you. You typically find that your size is way too popular. You, my friend, have just created a missed opportunity. The retailer lost a guaranteed sale because it didn't have your size. You leave the store and eventually find a similar look elsewhere. However, the damage is done. The second choice is just that: not your first choice. You drive home feeling annoyed with the retailer. Not only has the retailer missed an opportunity to sell, but it has also created a negative customer experience.

Thus far, we have discussed how we can leverage analytics to increase accuracy and optimize inventory of merchandise financial plans to plan key departments in line with seasonality and trends. We've also discussed how to tackle location clustering, leveraging an analytical approach to further localize and account for shifts in demand as a result of the omnichannel strategy and ever-evolving digital landscape. From there, we discussed leveraging these clusters to understand and keep up with the ever-changing true customer preferences with the use of analytics and additional data elements from social media, enabling the movement from product-centric to customer-centric assortment selections. We can have the best assortment to satisfy customers, but if we do not have their size, we lose. All of that work is thrown out the door. Now let's talk about how we are able to leverage analytics to take the assortment to the next step: size optimization.

Traditionally, retailers look at a higher level of the merchandise and location hierarchy to determine performance and contribution of sales by size. This, for example, could include looking at the total dress category across the highest level of location hierarchy to analyze the percentage contribution to sale for each size. They then use this information to create their size scale. "Size scale" is a term that describes the amount retailers should buy of each style-color by size as well as how much each location should receive. There are two reasons to avoid looking at historical sales performance at the chain. The first, more obvious reason is that not all stores are alike. As we mentioned, stores can have very different customers, varying by preference, demographic, and size. However, when you are working with over 50 stores, the process of analyzing size demand becomes incredibly hard to manage. So retailers resort to looking at a chain. The level of data when looking at store-level style-color and size sales performance is a large amount of data for the human eye to consume.

The second issue is the data that retailers are using to determine this size scale. Utilizing historical point-of-sale data does not give insight into true customer demand. Quite frankly, if you didn't receive the size, then the historical sales data will tell you that you didn't sell it and therefore you do not need it. You've created a loser loop. To defeat this issue, retailers may look at stock to sales. "Stock to sales" is a term that describes analyzing the size performance contribution to the inventory ownership contribution. If the chain is outselling a size compared to its inventory ownership, then this may give insight in to missed opportunity. But again, this goes back to the first challenge. When looking at the chain level, there may be stores that are under or over and net out to be equal.

We can leverage big data compute as well as analytics to overcome these challenges and help retailers win the sale and create a great customer experience. The term "big data compute" refers to the ability to calculate large amounts of data, so large that it would be impossible for an end business user to attempt. The other aspect here is the use of imputation techniques. Imputation sounds like a word out of your high school biology or genetics textbook, but don't be scared. In statistics, it's the process of replacing missing data with values. In this example, imputation is replacing missing sales due to a lack of inventory.

Each time a store sells out of a size, it creates what is referred to as an out of stock. When stores are out of stock of items, missed opportunities for sales can arise. Sometimes this concept is referred to as lost sales. However, more advanced statistical imputation techniques can create a much more accurate result. For example, being able to take into account when in the product life cycle a stock-out occurred gives a much more intelligent perspective than a traditional lost sales calculation. A lost sales calculation is typically replacing a missed opportunity with the location's average sale of the item. However, if the location did not have inventory on hand, then determining where in the product life cycle the stock-out took place is the next step. If the item was at a meaningful point in the life cycle, then the lack of inventory could have affected the demand. This means that if the item was about to be marked down to clearance the next day, the fact that the item was out of stock is actually a good thing. However, an item being out of stock during the beginning stages of the life cycle weighs more on the effect of the demand.

There are a plethora of different techniques for imputation. One imputation technique that can be leveraged is by utilizing location clustering. Earlier in the chapter we discussed clustering stores based on similar selling patterns of product to create groups of stores or even trade areas that have similar merchandise preferences. Buyers leverage these clusters or groups to efficiently create product assortments that tie to each cluster's merchandise demand. This aids in efficiently localizing assortments as well as becoming more customer centric. When stores are more customer centric, they are creating product assortments that are more tied to what customers are showing they are attracted to rather than retailers attracting customers to the retailers' idea of an assortment.

Clustering is also leveraged in understanding the true size demand. Stores can be clustered based on similar size selling. Like product selling or merchandise preferences, size selling can vary drastically. Two stores within 10 miles of each other could have a completely different size selling demand. For example, one store may sell more small sizes than the other store. This size selling can even be related to customer demographics within the area. Certain ethnicities or ages have different size demand; looking at the demographics of a local trade area can explain why the demand may vary.

When it comes to clustering stores based on similar size selling patterns, retailers can look at how a store sells down to the size level rather than the style-color or item level for assortment planning. These clusters can be completely different from the clusters that were used in assortment planning; that's completely acceptable. Once we have clusters of locations that sell sizes similarly, we can leverage these in imputation techniques.

One approach is to understand what the true missed opportunity of sales were based on a lack of inventory. Just because a store did not have the inventory does not necessarily mean that it would have sold it if they had it. Oftentimes, this is the issue with lost sales calculations. Lost sales calculations are based on an average week's sales units. If the store sells two units on average and it was out of stock, then the lost sale would be two units. However, that is not always the case.

The demand can fluctuate based on the day or week and other factors. These imputation techniques then look at a location's inventory. If the location was out of stock, then looking at stores that had similar size selling patterns gives insight into whether the specific location would have sold the item if it was in stock. If the similar stores did not sell the inventory at all for that given day, days, or weeks, then more than likely the location in question would have not sold any units if it had the inventory. This information helps to truly determine the best approach to imputation or understanding how to replace missing values of inventory with associated sales. This type of analytical calculation for true missed opportunity can be leveraged throughout the assortment management process. Most important, this analytical capability can give insight into what the store's true size selling curve would have been if it had the inventory to support the sales.

For example, let's say a store sold out of size smalls for a week of a specific black, bodycon fashion dress. The store sells an average of two units a week. The traditional lost sales calculation would determine that the store had a lost sales of two units. However, the average was two units, and the peak timing during the six weeks of the life cycle of the product was six units. For the given week in question that the store had zero units on hand, stores that have the same similar selling patterns did not sell any of the black, bodycon fashion dress either. Therefore, this location's true size demand for that time period would have been zero as well. These advanced imputation techniques require advanced analytical capabilities to increase the precision of understanding the true potential of size demand and more accurately predict the demand for the future.

Having the revised demand created by the advanced imputation techniques and taking into account the missed opportunities enables retailers to have a view of true customer preferences. This type of analysis can also be done at various levels in the location hierarchy. So retailers are able to have a true view of customer preferences for each one of their locations. The roll-up of these locations enables merchants to have a more accurate scaling by size when placing orders. The location-level detail can also be integrated into allocation to ensure that once the product arrives, it is sent to each store's size-level demand profile.

Being able not only to buy the product in a more accurate size range but also to execute to the demand by each location enables retailers to gain a substantial amount of revenue. It is actually one of the quickest ways that retailers can see improvement and justify the return on investment of the size scaling analytical solution. Having a more accurate size distribution helps reduce clearance because people are actually able to find their size. Increasing a retailer's in-stock position on sizes and ensuring the size distribution is the true size demand for that location enables retailers to reduce markdowns. Reducing item markdowns enables retailers to sell at higher price points and preserve margin. Ensuring the assortment has been optimized down to the size level based on the true size demand to each location increases sales profitability and ensures a good customer experience.

CHAPTER **4**

Fulfillment

ALLOCATION

Once the assortment has been planned down to the size level, the next step in the process is fulfilling the store inventory need, which is referred to as allocation. The term "allocation" is defined as the process of distributing inventory to the retail locations and fulfillment centers in an effort to fulfill future customer demand, whether it be in store or online. Allocation is one of the most critical pieces of the process. The goal of allocation is to ensure the right product is going to the right stores, at the right time to optimize inventory investments to maximize profitable sales, reduce missed opportunities, and avoid having to mark inventory down to clearance.

Once a buyer places an order with a vendor, also referred to as a purchase order, the vendor then either sends the inventory to the retailer's distribution center or directly to the retail locations. The decision to send products to certain locations is based on a handful of factors and also depends on the retailer's process. The first factor is the initial vision of the merchant's assortment plan. As you will recall, assortment plans are typically planned by clusters of locations and a vision of the assortment the buyer was curating. Therefore, allocation is executing to this vision by sending the product to these locations either once the inventory arrives at the distribution center or before the vendor sends the inventory directly to the retail locations.

The initial allocation of the product may be distributed according to the assortment plan or it may be distributed according to the location's need. Allocating to a location's need is where analytics can come into play. The need for product is established based on a calculation, which can vary in complexity. The calculation of a location's inventory need is called an allocation method. Typically, retailers have more than one method of allocation, depending on the product, allocation type, and time period.

There are four fundamental components of an allocation need calculation. The first component is the level of the merchandise hierarchy that will be utilized for the need calculation. For example, the location need may be derived from the total dress category in an allocation method for an initial allocation of dresses but at the specific style-color level for a fill-in allocation to fill back in to the sales performance of a specific style-color of dress.

The second component of an allocation need calculation is the version of sales data that will be leveraged. The historical point-of-sale data is a version of data, as is statistical forecasted sales data. Historical point-of-sales data is typically stored in three buckets: regular price, markdown price, and total sales. The regular price sales are the units that were sold at the regular ticket or promotion price. The markdown sales are the units that were sold at clearance prices and therefore have a lower margin. The total sales are the regular price sales plus the markdown sales lumped into one bucket. Regular price sales is the more ideal bucket of sales because these are the most profitable sales and are sold at the early stages of the product life cycle. These sales depict customer preferences much more accurately.

Unfortunately, not all retailers store these buckets of data. They may only be able to see total sales, which in essence would be allocating back to prior mistakes. A store may appear high in sales at the total sales level but, in fact, 95% of the sales could have been at clearance prices that were extremely low in gross margin. Therefore, one of the first steps in improving allocation methodologies is to begin storing and leveraging the regular price sales data.

In addition to historical point-of-sales data, retailers can leverage statistical forecasted sales data. Statistical forecasted sales data is the most optimal version to leverage because it takes into account trends, seasonality, outliers, holiday shifts, and the effects of causal factors, such as price changes and promotions. These forecasts can also be created at multiple levels of the hierarchy, which enables retailers to allocate to the true future demand rather than to history. Leveraging forecasted demand is much more accurate than using historical sales.

The third component of an allocation need calculation is the time period. This time period defines the historical or forecasted sales values that will be leveraged for a specific time. These time periods can be dynamic or static and can be previous or future time periods. Static time periods are periods of the time hierarchy that do not change. Dynamic time periods change over time. An example of this may be leveraging the last six weeks of sales. Each week, this exact time period changes and moves up a week, which is why it is defined as dynamic.

The time period can also be looking at the past or the future. Looking at the past would be our example of looking at the last six weeks of sales. Future time periods are looking ahead. For example, let's say today is January 1, 2017. If a purchase order is being allocated to arrive in the stores for February, then we can define February as the future time period. The historical sales would then be the February sales from 2016 or the statistically forecasted sales for 2017. Time period is a critical component of allocation because looking at past sales may not capture future seasonality.

Seasonality is a very important factor to consider in the time period component, especially by store. "Seasonality" is defined as patterns that occur every calendar year and are predictable. For example, every year Florida experiences an increase in traffic after Thanksgiving and through Easter. This is because a large number of people who live in the northern states migrate to Florida to escape the cold weather back home. Many of these individuals are retired. We refer to these individuals as "snowbirds." They flock down every year, and therefore sales consistently increase for this time period. Certain areas in Florida, such as Fort Myers and the southwest coast, experience a much larger increase in sales than others.

Therefore, if an allocation method component of time is not looking at the future demand in February, it would not take into account this large increase in demand. As a result, the stores would not get enough inventory. If they do not receive enough inventory to support their sales, then the retailer will experience a missed opportunity in sales and the customer experience would be reduced. On the flip side, when the snowbirds flock home after Easter, demand significantly decreases. If past time periods of the performance over the last six weeks were used for an allocation in May, then a store may receive way too much inventory. If this occurs, then the inventory will just sit there and not sell, because the demand is just not there anymore. Eventually this product would go to clearance, and the retailer would lose money.

Once we have defined the level of the merchandise that we will leverage, the sales data version of historical or forecasted sales, and the time period, the fourth component is the allocation method. Retailers could have one allocation or many. These methods vary based on store inventory need. Examples of allocation methods are allocating to: an assortment plan, a location financial plan, sales performance, sales contribution, targeted weeks of supply (WOS), an inventory targeted sell through percentage, and many other variations.

These methods leverage the historical or forecasted future demand of the defined time period, current inventory, and a series of calculations that vary in complexity to eventually arrive at a recommended allocation quantity by store. Let's talk through an example of a WOS allocation method. We have a dress purchase order coming into the distribution center to support the February sales. We've defined that for our fashion dresses, we would like all stores to own eight WOS. "WOS" describes how many weeks it would take to sell all of the inventory. Fashion items, for example, may have a life cycle of eight weeks. In that case, we would want to ensure that the store has enough inventory to continually support eight future weeks of sales. The ideal number of weeks that an item lives on the floor also varies by retailer; it is not necessarily eight weeks across the board. The WOS calculation is the average weekly sales divided by the inventory. So if store A does an average of 10 units of sales every week during the months of February and March and the store currently has 20 units, then it has only two WOS.

If our allocation method is to allocate a fashion dress purchase order to get all stores to an eight WOS, the method would look at each store's future average weekly sale of fashion dresses and determine how much each store would need to get to eight weeks. Store A in our example would need 80 units since the store sells an average of 10 a week. The allocation method typically takes into account how much inventory the store already has on hand as well as what is in transit to the store currently. "In transit" means it is either on a truck or preallocated to arrive to the store within the time frame that we are allocating. So in our example, if store A did not have any units of dresses on order, then it would need 70 units because 80 units minus their current 10 is 70 units.

However, most buyers enforce presentation minimums and maximums. The minimum is the least amount a buyer would ever want a store to receive. Typically this amount may be a size run or a minimum to make an impactful presentation. The maximum is the maximum amount that a buyer would want any one store to receive. For example, a buyer probably would not want one store to receive 70 units of a fashion dress.

One fixture typically holds 96 units, so 70 units would almost be an entire fixture of one specific style-color of a fashion dress. Yikes!

These presentations are important because, from a visual merchandising perspective, they must look appealing and draw the customer in. They entice customers to make the purchase. Think about it. Say you walk into a store and find a dress that you like somewhat but are not sure whether you like it enough to buy. If there was three-fourths of a fixture with the product, you would probably pass, because you know that the dress will still be there once you decide. However, if a smaller number is available, you probably would be more inclined to purchase the dress because you would not want to take the chance that it would not be there when you come back.

Once each store's inventory need is calculated, the presentation minimums and maximums are typically applied. The stores are also prioritized to determine which ones will receive the units off of each purchase order because there may not be enough units to fill each store's need. There may also be too many units on an order. Retailers handle this scenario in two ways: They either hold back inventory in their warehouse or distribution center for when the inventory is needed or they prioritize stores on which ones are most likely to sell the item and how much it costs to carry that item in the stores.

In addition to the allocation methods, there are three different types of allocation processes: postallocations, preallocations, and direct-to-store allocations.

In postallocations, vendors send the inventory to the retailers' distribution centers to be allocated. On average, this is probably the most common allocation process. In preallocations, the allocations are first done and then vendors pack the order by location, then send these location-specific boxes to the retailers' distribution centers. This preallocation process reduces time to store from initially receiving the inventory because it is already allocated and ready to go. These orders are quickly moved through the distribution center and are ready to be packed on the trucks to deliver to the stores. In direct-to-store orders, vendors send the inventory directly to the individual store based on an allocation they receive from retailers. A direct-to-store order reduces time to store even more than a preallocation because it bypasses the trip to the distribution center.

However, there are pros and cons to each process, and not all vendors offer all three process types. In addition to three different types of allocation *processes*, there are two different types of allocations: initial allocations and fill-in allocations. Initial allocations are products that have not yet been in the stores. With fill-in allocations, the product has already been on the floor, and additional inventory is sent to stores to replenish stock levels and enable locations to sell additional units to customers, or the product is being expanded to additional stores.

For initial allocations, all three processes can be leveraged. The only thing that may hinder the accuracy of allocations in preallocations and the direct-to-store allocation process is how far out the vendor needs the store allocation. When the allocation is done closer to the time that the product is expected to arrive in the stores, most up-to-date trends, inventory position, and inventory need can be calculated. If an allocation must be done three months before the product actually arrives, there is a potential to miss out on capturing a store that may have begun trending up in sales or experiencing a decline.

The same goes for fill-in allocations. The closer in time that the allocation can be done, the easier it is to capture more accurate and better sales trends. Recall that a fill-in allocation is typically a reorder of items that have already been in the store or an expansion to additional stores. The buyer may reorder a product if it is performing very well and therefore the stores need more product inventory to maximize sales. Reorders also occur if a buyer anticipates that the item will perform well and plans to flow more inventory in after the initial set is sold. Reorders also help when having to meet vendor minimums. If a vendor has a minimum unit requirement of 3,000 units but the retailer only has 50 stores, then each store would have to get an average of 60 units. Bringing 1,500 units in for the initial setup and an additional 1,500 units after a few weeks of sales enables the retailer to meet the minimum without drowning the stores with inventory or sacrificing presentations.

However, timing the flow of a reorder is critical. If the reorder arrives at the distribution center to be allocated and the initial product has not yet made it to the stores, then the allocation is extremely difficult because you oftentimes have to force inventory into locations that may not need it at the time. The need calculation will have to be determined based on a higher level of inventory need in the hierarchy, and the buyer misses the opportunity to gauge which stores are selling it well. If presentation maximums are enforced, then inventory may be forced to lower-performing stores due to the high-volume stores already owning the maximum amount of inventory desired. Forcing inventory into lower-volume stores may create excess inventory, which would become clearance or markdown and sell at a lower profit margin Allocating reorders with few to no sales also requires an intelligent allocation method to understand which locations are the most likely to sell the additional units. Other retailers are able to hold these orders in their warehouses or distribution centers until the stores have had ample time to sell the items; therefore, the units can be allocated to the stores most likely to sell additional units. This is the ideal scenario for fill-in allocations, but not all retailers have the ability, process, or bandwidth to utilize this type of hold-back model.

As you can see, allocation is a complex process, but it is also critical to the business. Allocation analyst is typically an entry-level position. Many times the allocation analyst is fresh out of college, and it may be his or her first job. My first job in corporate retail was as an allocation analyst, and I loved it! I will admit, though, that it is an extremely important job that can be intimidating as a first position. Not all retailers are at the same level of maturity in allocation. The most advanced retailers utilize analytical software, which enables the allocation process and methods to be predefined. When the methodology is predefined, the allocation analyst, planner, and buyer create a vision of the assortment as well as the allocation strategy, sales data that will be leveraged, time period, and need calculation. These components are then defined in the allocation parameter tables so that once the allocation arrives, the process is automated, efficient, and, most important, accurate in driving the right inventory to the right place at the right time. This ensures that the goal of allocation is met to optimize inventory investments to maximize profitable sales, reduce missed opportunities, and avoid having to mark inventory down.

However, some retailers have not yet reached this point and still are leveraging green-screen computer systems, which are terminals that display a black screen with green characters, homegrown allocation systems, or very basic allocation systems that require analysts to pretty much allocate manually. Analysts may prioritize stores themselves, considering few data elements, such as only total sales units or dollars. But as the world of retail evolves, many retailers are faced with doing more with less. Less inventory to drive more sales is a constant struggle. Making the most of the inventory you have is key to optimization. Archaic ways of allocating are not meeting today's pressures, and it makes little sense to entrust millions of dollars in inventory to someone with little experience.

As a result, many retailers are moving toward analytical allocation solutions to automate these processes. Retailers are also beginning to infuse more advanced analytics into their current allocation solutions. Implementing allocation software can be costly as well as a large change management for retailers. If a retailer already owns a software solution and has automated the allocation process but is seeking more accuracy in allocations, demand predictions, and customer preferences, infusing analytics into the current software solution can be a quick win.

A statistical forecast is a great example of an analytical approach that can be integrated into retailers' current solution to increase accuracy and return on investment. Many companies say they offer statistical forecasting. But when it comes down to it, their models just do not cut it for the complexity of retail. Some companies really offer trends applied to last year and call it statistical forecasting. Or their forecasts may take into account trends and seasonality but not causal factors, such as price changes or promotions in addition to holiday shifts and events.

Advanced forecasting capabilities can be sourced either as a service or by leveraging an advanced statistical forecasting platform, which can then be integrated into the current allocation software solution. Then the allocation analyst would be able to allocate using forecast sales rather than last year's sales. At the end of the day, it is all just data. Data generated from one solution can be easily made available in another solution, which is why infusing analytics into current allocation solutions can be extremely advantageous for retailers.

ORDER FULFILLMENT

In addition to referring to filling store inventory needs, the term "fulfillment" also refers to the process of meeting a customer's specific order need. Now that customers are able to shop through multiple touchpoints, including in-store, mobile apps, websites, and even some forms of social media, it is critical to leverage the most optimal fulfillment methodology. Often, order fulfillment is done through fulfillment centers. However, many retailers are moving toward in-store fulfillment in order to maximize inventory and support the brick-and-mortar locations. As sales transition from one outlet to the other, retailers must adjust their operations to continue to keep brick-and-mortar locations open and profitable.

Traditionally, an order from an e-commerce sale may have come from a fulfillment center or a store location. Determining the fulfilling location begins in a very basic logic and business rules approach. A business rule typically is in the form of an if-then statement. The least mature approach is to fulfill each item from the location that has the most on hand. In this example, the business rule would be: If the location has the highest inventory on hand, then fulfill from that location. This helps reduce the likelihood that the location will sell out prior to picking the items from the floor and packing them for shipping. However, there are many issues with this approach. The first issue is the fact that typically the stores that have the most inventory on hand in the beginning of the product life cycle are large-volume stores that received large quantities to meet the demands of customers walking into the locations. The other issue is that this approach does not take into account inventory productivity.

A slightly more advanced fulfillment process is to look at inventory productivity when determining the location to fulfill the order. For example, you can select the store that has the highest weeks of supply. Recall, a weeks-of-supply measure is the number of weeks it would take to sell the units. In this case, the store that would take the longest to sell through the product would be selected. This definitely helps select a location that is least likely to sell it from in-store purchases. However, fulfilling from inventory on hand and inventory productivity are not the most optimal approaches. Shipping fees vary based on the size of the shipment as well as the distance. So an e-commerce order could be possibly fulfilled from a store across the country when, in fact, the local store had the inventory on hand. Leveraging geographical radiuses is an additional component to truly maximizing shipping costs to retailers.

Besides inventory productivity and geographical radius, the number of items in the specific order must be considered. Not taking into account the number of items that are able to be fulfilled from one location can hurt the customer experience. Imagine you purchase five items online for a cruise that you are planning to go on next month. You've cruised online (no pun intended) checking out different sites, and you finally decide on a couple of swimsuits and a towel from one site. At checkout, you realize that one item is on backorder. Of course, it is your favorite item, but the backorder date is still within the timing of your window. So you decide to continue and pay the additional charge for expedited shipping in order to get the backordered item in time. In two days, you receive one box that has one piece of your order from one distribution center. The next day, you receive a box in the morning with one item from an additional store that fulfilled the item. Later that afternoon, you receive a box with two items from your local store. You are annoyed that the items came piecemeal and not all at once. Not to mention the fact that your dog goes absolutely crazy at each knock on the door and your infant, who hasn't slept in days, eventually falls asleep in time for the UPS delivery person to knock. But you remind yourself that vacation is around the corner and you push forward; after all, you love your new items.

The day before your cruise you pack your suitcase. In the process, you realize that your favorite swimsuit that was on backorder has yet to arrive. Of course, you log in to your app to track the shipment. The tracking information says it will not arrive for an additional four days. How can that be? You paid for expedited shipment. So you immediately call customer service. You are told that if you had wanted the backordered item to be shipped expedited, you would have had to pay an additional fee and have needed to call customer service to arrange once your order was confirmed because the site does not enable this additional shipping arrangement. Not only did you receive your order in multiple boxes, but you also did not receive it all in time.

The retailer has just lost a lifetime customer. One bad experience can completely turn off customers, and retailers can potentially lose a lot of business. Not to mention the fact that today's customers are very vocal on social media. Millennials rely on word of mouth and their friends' opinions when determining brands and retailers to shop. Therefore, customer experience and the amount of individually shipped boxes are critical components in addition to inventory productivity and geographical radiuses. Selecting the location that is not only close in distance to the customer but also able to fulfill multiple items if not the entire order is essential to creating a positive customer experience and keeping shipping fees down for retailers. In the scenario just described, the customer paid the shipping fees, but because the shipment came in multiple boxes from various locations and distribution centers, the shipping cost to the retailer was actually more than the customer paid. The website also did not fully explain the process of backorders and did not enable customers to expedite shipping of a backorder.

This is where intelligent fulfillment becomes critical to retailers. Shipping fees are hot topics for the C-suite. The main mission of a retailer is to continue to drive profitability. But in today's changing digital landscape, profitability has become an obstacle that retailers are trying to figure out. Traditional fulfillment processes are not cutting it. An analytical approach is critical to reducing costs and increasing customers' positive experiences in order to gain their loyalty. An intelligent fulfillment strategy can leverage inventory productivity, geography, all items in the order to fulfill, the likelihood that the location will have the inventory available once a store associate receives the order, and other factors.

Today's retailers are not much concerned with the real-time decisions and analytical approach to offer customer incentives, although this area will become more important in the future. An example would be leveraging an analytical optimization engine. A true analytical optimization engine enables all of these components to be taken into account and run through all of the different scenarios to select the most optimal fulfillment strategy to reduce fulfillment costs while also protecting brick-and-mortar sales opportunities. Say the result of an assessment shows that the shipping fees in the most optimal situation will still cost the retailer; customers can be offered incentives, such as discounts or percentages off, if they pick the order up in-store.

Take, for example, large items such as grills or refrigerators. Let's say an online promotion of free shipping with a certain purchase amount is offered to customers. However, it will cost the retailer a large amount to ship a grill for free. Leveraging a real-time decision based on analytical optimization would recommend an additional promotion to entice the customer to pick up the item in-store. Not to mention the fact that most customers purchase additional items when picking up in-store. I know I can never resist, especially at Target, with the bargain area right in the front of the store.

Retailers are faced with leveraging analytical approaches to strategically fulfilling e-commerce purchases. This approach increases top-line sales, profitability by reducing shipping costs, and positive customer experiences, which truly are the main missions of retailers.

CHAPTER 5

Pricing

etail Systems Research reported in its "Pricing 2015: Learning to Live in a Dynamic, Promotional World" benchmark report that the top three strategic pricing challenges are increased price sensitivity, increased aggressive competitor pricing, and increased price transparency. How many times have you found an item that you wanted badly but just couldn't stomach the price? But the amount that you are willing to pay also depends on the product and the situation. Big-ticket items tend to be researched a bit more than tank tops, for example. You cruise online, check Amazon, and hunt for the best deal. The whole fad of extreme couponing has even become a sport. Coupons traditionally were in newspapers. Now there are websites dedicated to sharing coupons. Outlet and discount stores are also on the rise, and many large retailers are opening outlet stores.

The economy took a hit when the housing market crashed in 2008. Many U.S. citizens found themselves upside down on their houses. The following year, gas prices spiked and unemployment rates rose. According to the U.S. Bureau of Labor Statistics, the unemployment rate was 4.6% in January 2007; in January 2010, the rate had more than doubled at 9.8%. Many Americans owed more money on their houses than they were worth and also found themselves let go from their jobs or struggling to afford the gas to get to their jobs. Consumer spending was affected, as was customers' perceptions of price. Consumer spending took a dip but then slowly increased over the last 10 years.

While consumer spending has slowly grown after the housing market crash, customer perception of price is still the same as it was during the recession. The perception or sensitivity to price is still very high. Price is an emotional decision for individuals. People love bargains. They love to feel like they have found a deal, and they take it personally when they think they've been overcharged or ripped off. Think about a time when you purchased an item from a store, such as a nice handbag or pricey pair of shoes. The next week, imagine walking into the same store and seeing the item on sale for 50% off. It is always gut wrenching and frustrating, and pulls at your emotions. Individuals who have gone through a difficult economic situation are much more sensitive to price than individuals who are not impacted by an economic crash.

Yet there is also a difference in pricing perception across generations. Millennial spending is on the rise as the millennial population becomes a larger portion of the workforce. By 2020, millennials will represent 50% of the workforce, rising to 70% by 2030. These individuals will continue to increase in the percentage of consumer spending. According to the 2015 Nielsen Global Corporate Sustainability Report, 73% of global millennials do not mind paying extra for a brand that gives back to a good cause. Millennials are also known for spending more on experiences than products, unless, of course, it is the latest iPhone or tech gadget. The differing emotional ties to product pricing between generations and even at a customer level have retailers shaking their heads in confusion.

In addition to customers' perception of price and understanding millennials' spending habits, the advent of the Internet completely transformed the retail industry and the way we think of shopping. The growth of mobile and technology has also revolutionized the industry and created additional complexities and challenges for retailers in pricing.

"Channel" is a term retailers use to describe the mechanism by which customers shop and retailers connect with their customers. As discussed in Chapter 1, omnichannel is the mechanism that retailers use to interact with customers through touchpoints such as in-store, mobile websites, and social media. The term "digital landscape" is also used to describe the mix of channels.

Due to the increase in channels, retailers are adjusting their business processes as well as their technology to support these initiatives. As e-commerce sales continue to grow, store volume declines. While online growth is rapidly increasing, the majority of sales are still taking place in physical (brick-and-mortar) locations. The average online sales represent 16% of a retailer's total sales. But it is becoming increasingly difficult to distinguish between online sales and in-store sales. Often customers cruise through sites prior to purchasing online or surf competitor sites for products.

The rise over the years in omnichannel has created an enormous increase in competition. Now that the competition is everywhere, price comparisons can be done with a click of a button on your iPhone. Some retailers are even offering to match prices from competitors with price comparisons on their mobile devices. Black Friday is a promotional event that earned its name in the 1950s. Factory managers actually coined the term because of the large number of workers who would call out sick the day after Thanksgiving. People would travel into cities from all over to start their holiday shopping on this day each year. The term then evolved to describe the massive amount of crowds and chaos in the stores. In the 1980s, the term was leveraged to describe the beginning of a retailer's balance sheet moving from red to black. This movement from red to black illustrates the seasonal beginning of holiday sales and increased revenue.

Black Friday grew to become a shopping holiday over the years. This event became a staple for U.S. families and has since evolved due to online sales. Cyber Monday is the Monday after the Thanksgiving holiday, and this day has become the largest online sales day of the year. Cyber Monday deals were created to entice customers to continue the shopping-filled weekend into the next week, but the day soon came to compete with Black Friday. The two holidays have become a battle between in-store and online offers. Retailers have to work harder than ever to stay in the game. The struggle to compete with e-commerce retailers such as Amazon has left many retailers out of business. Retailers that play in both worlds need to wrestle with a pricing model that competes with online pricing but that also takes into account the different costs associated with selling products in physical locations.

Omnichannel has not only expanded the competitive playing field, it has also created an expectation of free shipping. Customers expect product to be available whenever and wherever. Think about the last time you couldn't find your size of an item that you loved. Of course there was a huge sense of disappointment, but the next best thing is having the item shipped to your home. No one is going to be okay with paying an additional shipping fee on the item.

A good example of a retailer that has an effective approach is Nordstrom Rack. The Nordstrom Rack app has been designed so that you can try on items. If you cannot find your size, all you have to do is scan the barcode of a different size. The app leverages real-time data in the store to inform you whether your size is in fact somewhere in the store that you are currently shopping in. If it is not, you can order the item and have it shipped to your home with a click of a button and free shipping.

This expectation of free shipping has created tension on order fulfillment as well as profitability. Each box that is shipped to a customer's home costs money. Depending on the retailer, there could be multiple boxes shipping from various destinations, which only increases the shipping fees. Also, the expectation of fast shipping speed is on the rise. Once Amazon Prime launched with its offer of free two-day shipping, the standards were set. I personally cannot stand ordering items online with a ship date of more than two to three business days. These business days are like waiting for Santa to come but for days instead of a single eve.

These changes in the retail industry, marketplace, and customer have created challenges for retailers. They now have to become much more strategic in their pricing strategies in order to balance staying competitive, growing market share, and increasing profitability. Retailers must tackle multiple types of pricing strategies, from varying item types to the life cycle of each product. There are three phases of this life cycle: preseason, in-season, and end of season. Often retailers leverage four seasons: spring, summer, fall, and winter. "Preseason" is defined as the early stages of the merchandise life cycle, prior to the season starting. Often retailers create assortment plans and pricing strategies prior to the products arriving in stores. Retailers may also bring items in prior to the start of the season to ensure that the product arrives at the stores early. During preseason planning, the regular price of items—the price on the item ticket or tag—is established. In retail, this price typically is one that is not changed once the product reaches the store. In grocery or hardware stores, items are often reticketed. It takes a lot of manpower to reticket a large number of items, so typically retailers avoid it when possible.

"In-season" is defined as the merchandise life cycle during its affiliated season, such as jackets in winter and swimwear in summer. In-season planning typically takes place once the product begins to arrive at locations and sales start to occur. In-season, retailers move and groove to business risks and trends. Promotional pricing is leveraged and planned in-season. "Promotional price" is the price of the item that helps drive sales and traffic. These prices are temporary price reductions and can fluctuate. Retailers adjust promotional pricing throughout the season, depending on how the item performs compared to the original plan.

The term "end of season" refers to the last cycle of the merchandise life. Items are typically promoted to drive sales and inventory productivity until they are marked down to clearance. "Markdown price" is the term used to define an item in the last stage of its life cycle. Very few items are left at the markdown price, and they are typically merchandised on the floor in a specific area. Some refer to this as clearance or a clearance zone. Managing the pricing strategy throughout the product life cycle is called life cycle pricing. Promotional and markdown pricing is a reduction of the regular or ticket price. Ensuring that the pricing strategy accounts for each phase in the life cycle is critical to successfully managing the product.

Pricing strategies and the pricing life cycle can vary by retailer as well as the different types of retailers, such as outlet stores, department stores, and specialty stores. Outlet stores typically buy items from vendors at low cost because they buy what is left over from a season or excess. Such buys often are called opportunity buys. These orders are typically a mixture of sizes and not necessarily a full size range. This structure gives customers a feeling of being on a treasure hunt. The pricing and the structure of price vary by retailer. Department stores have a different pricing model from outlet stores. Promotional department stores price items in a structure that enables them to promote the items. This gives customers a sense that they scored a deal. Outlet stores typically price the items at low prices with the original ticket price showing. However, both the promotional department store and the outlet store are leveraging customer emotions to draw them into a purchase by price.

In addition to pricing strategies varying by the type of retailer, strategies are also different by product type. Think about jackets. Jackets typically are brought into locations before the season starts, or preseason, and then are sold throughout the winter season. Toward the end of the season, jackets may be marked down to clearance. On the opposite side of the spectrum are items that do not have a specific selling season and tend to sell all year. These items are also typically not fashion items and have a much longer life. We typically refer to these as basics. Packs of Hanes white T-shirts, for example, sell all year and every year.

PRICING ANALYTICS

As the retail landscape has changed over the years, it has become increasingly difficult for retailers to maintain a consistent and coherent pricing strategy. Retailers must understand where they have to be competitive and where they may be able to squeeze out a little more profit. The goal is to determine what the prices should be. Developing a pricing strategy is about balancing the activity of retaining current customers, acquiring new customers, and increasing profitability. Customers want the best deal, but retailers have to keep their lights on and ensure that they continue to drive revenue.

Pricing can often be a fine line to straddle, and it can also make or break retailers. This is where retailers are leaning on analytics to help drive pricing decisions. Leading retailers are leveraging the power of big data, analytics, and automation to shape the future of pricing. The future of retail pricing encompasses not only the ability to leverage analytics to determine pricing and promotional strategies in the stores, it also requires determining the pricing strategies for all channels. These channels include brick and mortar, website, Twitter, Instagram, Facebook, and other retail touchpoints. Advanced analytical capabilities are now also enabling retailers to personalize pricing down to the customer level. Understanding how price and other components affect demand, such as trends, seasonality, and holidays, is the first step to creating optimized pricing strategies.

Price elasticity is the measure that represents the degree to which customers are sensitive to fluctuations in price. If price has fluctuated but demand has a small variation, then the item is inelastic. If demand has large variations, then the item is elastic. Price sensitivity historically has been a concept based on judgment and testing and measuring. Now price sensitivity can be statistically calculated. A very rudimentary calculation for price elasticity is the percentage change in demand divided by the percentage change in price. It sounds simple, but when you are trying to determine the price elasticity over time, for thousands of products, levels in the hierarchy, and then by location or customer segment, it becomes a challenge. So many factors and components affect fluctuations in demand, taking these concepts into account makes the calculation much more complex. For example, understanding the fluctuation in demand as a result of seasonality or events and holidays that are not price related creates a need for advanced statistical modeling.

In order to have a good picture of price elasticity, retailers must have the data. The data needed for price elasticity is historic prices over time as well as the demand and factors to account for holidays and events. Not all retailers store these prices over time in their databases. I often see retailers storing only one bucket of sales for an item. This one bucket of sales includes the sales that took place at regular price and/ or promotional pricing and then clearance by day or week. This set of data does not clearly differentiate when the item moved to clearance. Often demand varies once an item is marked down for clearance and moved to the clearance rack. Analysis becomes extremely difficult because the profitable and unprofitable sales are being lumped together in one bucket over time.

For this reason, the first step is data management and storing these prices and bucketing the sales appropriately. An example of this would be to store sales that occurred prior to being marked down to clearance in one column of data over time and then use a separate column of data for the clearance sales. Once the item is flagged as clearance, the inventory moves into the clearance inventory data, and the sales begin to populate the clearance column.

Also, this data can be stored at various levels in the location hierarchy, from total company to locations and all the way down to customer-level information for e-commerce as well as customer loyalty programs. The amount of data is also important. To calculate price elasticity, you need a minimum of a year's worth of data; two to three years gives the best picture. As retailers are moving toward more intelligent analytical pricing strategies, they may have to invest more time before they can utilize the prices and see a return on investment.

The data should also be stored at all levels of the merchandise hierarchy. For new items, there may not be any history. However, you can calculate price elasticity at different levels of the hierarchy. For example, all fashion dresses can be analyzed to understand how elastic the price of fashion dresses is rather than calculating it as total dresses. Think about it. Are you more likely to spend more money on a little black dress than a fashion dress? You would likely get more use out of the little black dress, so you are less sensitive to price for that item.

Alternate or dynamic hierarchies can be leveraged as well. A "hierarchy," by definition, is a ranking system where items are classified in different levels. Three different hierarchies are utilized in merchandising hierarchies: merchandise, location, and time. People in retail refer to this as MLT—merchandise, location, and time. The merchandise hierarchy naming and ordering convention can vary by retailer. Typically it starts at the top with the total company. This can be followed by division or category.

Typically, the standard hierarchy is static; it does not change during the course of the season. Changes made to this hierarchy require information technology resources, and they can be big undertakings. For example, say the static hierarchy has dresses as the lowest level and then all of the style-colors below it. If a buyer and/or planner wants to see dresses by casual and dressy or fashion versus basic, they would have to wait for the next reclassification of the hierarchy.

However, retailers could leverage an alternate or analytical hierarchy, or one that is outside of the standard hierarchy. These dynamic hierarchies leverage attributes to define and reorganize the data. An "attribute" is a characteristic of a hierarchical level. Attributes are used to describe levels of the merchandise and location hierarchy. Attributes are extremely useful in assortment management.

The concept of merchandise attributes, or analytical hierarchies, was covered in Chapter 3 when we discussed utilizing merchandise or location attributes to create assortment plans. For example, if a retailer's hierarchy is limited only to dresses and the lower levels are the actual styles, then we can use an attribute to characterize the items as fashion versus basic or career versus casual. We can then calculate the price elasticity at these levels to get a more accurate price effect.

Creating analytical hierarchies is definitely a mixture of art and analytics. We can leverage analytics to determine which attributes are driving the purchasing decisions to understand how to set up our analytical hierarchy. The amount of data at these levels is important to take into account. It is the law of large numbers. The more sales volume there is, the more accurate trends and seasonality predictions will be. But these hierarchies should be created in partnership with buyers to add the art and understand the future vision of the products.

Fluctuation in price is also key to understanding price elasticity. If the price never changes, it is difficult to predict what will happen if it does change. For example, if historically all dresses have been priced at $50, then it is difficult to understand what would happen if we price a handful of dresses at $60. Price elasticity is a critical component to determining pricing decisions in all price life cycles. The error rates are also correlated with how easy it is to understand and explain the data. Therefore, the more factors you can account for, the better the prediction.

This analytical approach is done in three steps, which is referred to as time-series decomposition. Time-series decomposition suggests that the data makeup consists of trends, seasonality, and irregular patterns. These irregular patterns can be caused by causal factors, such as promotions. The steps in the decomposition include a process to deseasonalize the data, determining the effects of causal factors on demand, and forecasting the demand. The first process is to deseasonalize the historical data at various analytical hierarchical levels. The term "deseasonalizing data" refers to the process of removing seasonality from historical demand values. This type of analytical approach can be determined at any level of the time hierarchy but most frequently is performed at the week level. Often data is deseasonalized based on the promotional planning calendar. For ease of explanation, we will use a monthly calendar example.

The first step to deseasonalize the data is to determine the centered moving average, which represents a typical sales volume centered on a specific level of time. For our example of leveraging months, this centered moving average would represent a typical month of sales volume aligned on the selected month. Then we calculate a ratio by taking the actual sales values for that specific time period and dividing it by the centered moving average to determine the percentage difference to the average. Let's say we are looking at June, and the average volume for January through

June and for July through December is 100 units of sales. The actual sales for July were 80 units. Therefore, the ratio would be 80 divided by 100, which is 0.80 or 80% of the typical month demand.

The next step is calculating the unadjusted factor. Adjusted factors are averages of each time period annually. In our example, we would average the July ratios over all of the historical sales that we have stored. For example, one year the ratio for July is 0.80, but the following year it is 0.90. If we average the two, the adjusted factor would be 0.85. Then we multiply the sale values for each time period by this adjusted factor to determine the deseasonalized data. So we would multiply 80 units by 0.85 to get 68 units. We perform this calculation for each level in the time hierarchy. The resulting deseasonalized data has now stripped out the seasonality, so we can get a more accurate picture of how other factors affect sales.

Once the data has been deseasonalized, the next phase of time-series decompensation is to determine the effects of causal factors and events on demand. Regression analysis is a statistical modeling process that estimates variable relationships and helps investigate the effects of certain factors on a target. There are various types of regression analysis. In this case, we want to understand the effect of causal factors to the target, which is sales. These causal factors can be holidays, events, and fluctuations in price. For areas such as fashion that have short life cycles, these price fluctuations are mainly at a category level or higher level in the merchandise hierarchy. For example, within dresses or casual dresses, it is understanding what the price elasticity is after normalizing the data for other impacts on demand such as inclusion in a circular, placement on display, events, holidays, and so forth.

Now we can perform regression analysis on the deseasonalized data to determine the effect of multiple factors. Regression analysis enables the calculation of the effect of a specific factor while also taking into account other factors that have influence. In price optimization, the key is to understand the impact and lift of adjusting a promotional price as well as the promotion offer type, such as a coupon, direct mailer, or flyer; being advertised on the cover or inside; promoting in-store as a buy one, get one event; and many more. Other factors that must be accounted for to determine demand are the product life cycle, cannibalization, halo effects, and inventory levels. The term "halo effects" refers to the tendency for one promotion to affect the sales of another. Take, for example, key lime pie. No one ever eats key lime pie without whipped cream! So when forecasting the demand for whipped cream, we must take into account the promotion of key lime pie. Halo effects can be tricky to understand.

Price elasticity can be calculated using different regression models. Think of a model as a calculation. Different calculations can generate price elasticity. Just as we talked about statistical forecasting, an error rate is generated from these models. R-squared is a typical error rate leveraged in price elasticity models. Statistical models with the lowest error rate are the best, most accurate models. R-squared is expressed as a decimal number. The closer the number is to 1, the more accurate the model. So, for example, if the R-squared of model A is .05 and the R-squared of model B is .98, then model B is the winning model.

By leveraging regression analysis, we have accounted for events such as holidays, sporting events, or marketing events as well as causal factors, such as the impact price fluctuations have on demand. The impact of price fluctuations on demand can be calculated using an analytical hierarchy with attributes. For example, we can leverage the attribute of fashion and basic dresses to understand how sensitive customers are to price for fashion dresses.

Once retailers understand price effects as well as how other factors influence demand, sales can be statistically forecasted. The statistical forecasting can also be done at various levels in the merchandise and location hierarchy. For example, leveraging fashion versus basic dresses to perform regression analysis and then leveraging the total dress category to forecast future demand is one way that retailers can utilize different levels of the hierarchy.

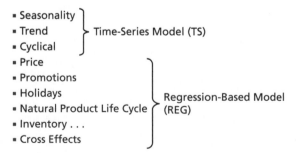

This is an example of using multiple models. We have used a regression model to determine the effect of events and causal factors at the dynamic hierarchy of fashion dresses versus basic dresses. We then used the total category of dresses to forecast the future demand, capturing trends and seasonality. We then combine these models to estimate the future demand of all levels. Using multiple models to calculate price elasticity and demand as two components acting separate from each other increases accuracy by determining how each component truly affects demand. We refer to this as multiplicative modeling. Advanced analytical software solutions can leverage multiplicative modeling techniques in an automated process. The SAS Institute has advanced statistical capabilities to support this type of process. This is an example of leveraging statistical modeling to support a business process. The solution analyzes the merchandise, the locations, and the time period to determine the most appropriate models as well as levels of the hierarchy that this analysis should be done in based on which level is most appropriate. The levels also include attribute levels, enabling analytical hierarchies to drive pricing strategies that are not restricted to the static hierarchy and may not incorporate the difference in how customers perceive price.

These forecasted sales, which take into account how factors affect demand, enable retailers to leverage optimization to determine the recommended and most optimal pricing strategy that aligns with business goals and initiatives. Optimization and scenario analysis can be leveraged throughout the product life cycle to determine the most appropriate pricing strategy. The analytical engine will run through different scenarios of price and apply the business rules, predict the outcome, and then select the most optimal price scenario. There could be hundreds of scenarios that would take an individual a ridiculous amount of time to go through. But a statistical engine automates this process and drastically reduces the time required to determine the optimal scenario. Depending on the point in time of the product's life, performance, and the business goals, additional factors to include in the optimization will adjust throughout the life cycle. The price at which an item sells directly affects how much gross margin, or profitability, the retailer will earn from the sale. Retailers look to drive the most optimal pricing as additional competition arises, costs of free shipping rise, and retailers' balancing act of retaining customers and acquiring new ones while driving profitability becomes trickier. Let's take a look at how these analytical components can be leveraged for each step in the merchandise and product life cycle.

REGULAR PRICE

The first price in the pricing life cycle is the regular price or ticket price. This price is important to get right because the next two price cycles can only go down; it is important to give the price enough room to move. This is why retailers think of it and plan it as a life cycle. The first component of planning a regular price is understanding what the cost to the retailer will be. The cost is just that. "Cost" is defined as the price a retailer has to pay the vendor for the items. Typically the regular price is higher than the cost; otherwise the retailer loses money. However, there are times when retailers will price lower than cost to get customers in the door. This cost price is also a part of the negotiation. The best buyers are the wheelers and dealers who try to get this price as low as possible. There may be a minimum quantity that must be purchased. We refer to this as vendor minimums. However, the more you buy, the more power you have in negotiation to get the costs lower. This is a great advantage for large retailers, like Walmart, which buys units for their over-4,000 stores in the United States. For smaller retailers or boutiques, even reaching vendor minimums can be challenging.

Once the cost is negotiated, the next component is to understand the price elasticity. Business rules, which are constraints to a pricing process, can be utilized. They are typically in the form of if-then statements. For example, many retailers leverage competitor pricing. Often retailers build in a business rule to say that if the competitor's price is lower than the calculated price, then make the price equal to that of the competitor's price. Retailers may not leverage this rule on all items. Analytics can aid in determining which items are statistically proven to be the most sensitive to competitor pricing through competitor elasticity or cross-item price elasticity. Cross-item price elasticity and competitor elasticity determine the sensitivity or fluctuation in demand as a result of changes in the price of a separate item. Cross-item price elasticity and competitor elasticity are also known as cannibalization.

This insight can determine which items retailers will leverage competitor pricing business rules.

Analytical solutions can perform optimization and scenario analysis with additional business rules, competitor data, and effects on demand from factors such as price fluctuation and events. The analytical engine will run through different scenarios of price and apply the business rules, predict the outcome, and then select the optimal price scenario. The analytical engine automates the analysis process and drastically reduces the time to determine the optimal scenario. The end result is a recommended regular price by item. Retailers then utilize this regular price as the base price for the rest of the pricing life cycle. Having the optimal regular price can drive profitable sales at the beginning of the life cycle and avoid excess inventory as well as markdowns or clearance.

PROMOTIONAL PRICING

Promotional activity is a tricky task to manage. Promotions often drive customers into stores and result in higher traffic and top-line sales. But there is a fine line between driving traffic and sales while also maintaining profitability and not giving everything away. Promotions come in many forms, such as a percentage off the regular price, a dollar amount off the regular price, buy one get one free (BOGO), and gifts with purchase (GWP).

Promotions are often leveraged for two main functions: as marketing vehicles to drive store traffic and as merchandising processes to sell through inventory. Marketers strive to increase traffic, retention, and attrition through marketing events. These events can be in the form of direct mailers, catalogs, flyers, radio and television promotions, as well as social media. Marketers strive to attract customers to the store or the website. Merchandisers strive to ensure that customers find the right assortment to increase sales. As described earlier, inventory has a certain life cycle, so it is critical for merchandising teams to sell through the inventory when originally planned. If sales of certain items start to slow down, there is less room to bring in new items to prepare for the next season. Therefore, merchandising teams leverage pricing strategies to drive customers to purchase and sell through inventory.

From the customer's perspective, promotions are drivers and emotional connections. As bargain hunting has evolved to become more like a sport, customers absolutely love coupons, promotions, and finding the best deal. Often I find myself using promotions as an excuse to buy items that I do not necessarily need but buy because the item was such a good deal.

Determining which items to promote, what type of promotion to use, and how much to promote is often very difficult. Retailers have a recurring ad planning process that consists of determining the items that will be promoted for marketing and advertising. During the recurring ad planning meetings, marketing and merchandising teams collaborate to determine what the themes should be, what items will be leveraged, and what the pricing should be. Retailers frequently use direct mailers or flyers. Themes consist of colleges, local sports, back to school, holidays, and others. Once the theme of the ad has been decided, the items that are leveraged are then determined along with the pricing strategies.

Retailers that hold storewide promotions, use coupons, or have customer loyalty incentives must consider additional factors. Marketing typically manages these overall store promotions, so collaboration between pricing and marketing is vital. If a buyer or planner is unaware that the marketing team is holding an in-store event, it could have a drastic effect on the overall performance and margin of the item that is being promoted.

For example, say an item with a regular price of $100 is being promoted at 50% off, so the selling price is $50. However, if the marketing team is holding an additional 30% off the entire store event, the $50 item would then be reduced to $35. This would result in the overall promotional discount for the item being 65%. As mentioned, buyers and planners have specific gross margin targets to achieve. Understanding all the components of the promotional activity within the store is crucial to determining the optimal item pricing in an effort to achieve gross margin targets. Promotional pricing and in-store events also occur on retailers' websites. Retailers hold specific online events, some of which may occur only for a certain time during a day. Historically, the merchandising and marketing business units operated in silos; today's retailers are seeing how important the collaboration of merchandising, marketing, and e-commerce is for their business.

The impact of marketing events also varies by product. For example, if marketing is offering a coupon in the newspaper this weekend, then the coupon will have an impact on sales and the selling price of products. Just as we discussed, understanding and taking into account the marketing promotions is critical to determining the most optimal and profitable promotion strategy for lower levels of the merchandise hierarchy. But the impact is not always the same across the business. Baby boomers read newspapers much more often than millennials. We may assume then that the coupon offered in the newspaper will have less of an effect on the sales of junior or young men's products. This assumption can be statistically qualified. Retailers typically store transaction-level data (or T-log, named to refer to logging of transactions). A "transaction" is each individual purchase. Each time customers swipe their card, shell out cash, or press the purchase confirmation button online, a transaction takes place. This data contains a wealth of information. Of course, the exact data elements vary by retailer, but typically this data includes each item purchased, the total dollar price paid for each item, the number of each item that was purchased, and whether a coupon was applied.

This T-log data can be leveraged to understand how likely customers are to apply a coupon to a transaction that contains certain product categories. Understanding the likelihood of coupon use for junior apparel, for example, can help determine the optimal price. If junior dresses were going to be promoted at 50% off and a mobile app coupon offered an additional 20% off an entire purchase, buyers would need to consider the likelihood that juniors would leverage the mobile coupon (which is much more likely than a newspaper coupon) and plan for that reduction. Therefore, the optimal price may be to offer dresses at 40% off instead of 50% off in order to protect the profitability of the sale.

Not many retailers are at a point where they are leveraging customer-level transaction data to determine coupon likelihood. As retailers utilize more advanced analytical pricing strategies and optimization, this deeper level of analysis will drive profitability and give them a better sense of what promotional activities and offers drive traffic.

Promotional management first began at the highest level of the location hierarchy; in other words, the promotions offered were the same for all customers shopping on a website and in all stores.

However, as retail has evolved and retailers look to be as profitable as possible, pricing strategies evolve as well. With advances in technology, retailers are now able to plan and manage promotions differently by location as well as for customers online. We discussed the concept of price elasticity earlier in the chapter. Price elasticity, or sensitivity to fluctuations in price, can be calculated at any level of the merchandise hierarchy as well as the location hierarchy. Retailers are now able to understand which locations or trade areas have higher price elasticities; this analysis can even go as precise as the customer level to offer personalized pricing promotions by understanding each customer's shopping behaviors on the retailer's website. Customer-level promotional decisions are usually based on propensity-to-respond models. These models determine how likely customers are to respond to certain promotional offer types, such as e-mail and coupons, as well as the promotional pricing that is offered. This type of modeling determines which customers would have bought the product regardless of the promotion versus the customers who actually purchased an item due to the promotion. This type of analysis helps retailers become more strategic in promotional spending to drive sales and profitability.

Determining the optimal promotional strategy down to a cluster of stores, store level, and even customer level requires data as well as scalable analytics. We are talking a lot of data here, so determining the optimal promotional strategy with large amounts of data requires heavy horsepower. Determining the level at which promotions will be managed is the first step in deciding on the strategy. We spoke in Chapter 4 about the concept of clustering trade areas based on similar selling patterns to leverage in creating assortment plans. We can also leverage clustering to cluster similar stores or customers based on their sensitivity to price. Think about it. Different areas of the country have different demographics, and the reaction and sensitivity to price is much different in these areas. Income levels have a high impact on price elasticity as well as the merchandise that is being sold. For example, items like school uniforms are essentials and therefore have lower elasticity than fashion tops. Fashion tops may be nice to have for certain income levels; if the price fluctuates to too high a price, customers may be less likely to buy in a specific cluster of locations but customers in other location clusters may not be affected. Retailers may apply additional constraints to account for cross shopping, and certain stores that are within a specific proximity may require the same pricing strategy.

Therefore, clustering stores based on similar price elasticity within a category of merchandise enables manageable localized pricing strategies. A maximum number of clusters may also be required by retailers to aid in efficiency. For example, perhaps a retailer can send out only three different versions of a flyer due to financial constraints or delivery capabilities. The retailer could use statistical clustering with cluster constraints to determine the appropriate customers or zip codes associated with each cluster for different flyer versions. Say a retailer can produce three different flyers for the month of August. One flyer consists of a back to school theme with children's clothing and a promotional coupon for the weekend prior to school starting. A second flyer consists of a college theme showing game-day merchandise. The last flyer consists of career clothing and essentials. Depending on customers' demographics and shopping patterns, they would get one of the three flyers that most relates to their profile.

The same concept can be leveraged at the customer level for e-commerce sales. Data is collected whenever customers create user accounts and log in on a retailer's website, browse the site, add items to their baskets, and purchase these items. Retailers know a lot more than you think about you. Your online shopping behavior can bring a wealth of knowledge about what drives your path to purchase and how sensitive you are to price as well as your propensity to respond to a promotional offer. This information can also be used to analytically cluster together customers into customer segments based on price sensitivity, propensity, and similar shopping patterns as well as demographic information. Customer segmentation is used for many marketing activities, which we discuss in Chapter 6.

Once the items were defined in the assortment plan, performance and productivity metrics were planned. These include key performance indicators, such as but not limited to sales dollars, sales units, gross margin, inventory sell through, and turnover. Once the items are delivered to the stores, promotional activities are leveraged as drivers to fulfill these plans. Depending on the retailer, this promotional activity may occur constantly or may be leveraged only under certain circumstances. For example, there are quite a few department stores that promote heavily. When customers shop at these stores, they hardly ever buy items at the regular ticket price. There is always some kind of promotion. These retailers take their promotional activity into account when determining the regular price. This approach can be very profitable because customers believe they are scoring great deals when they see the large reduction from the ticket price. However, it can also train customers to continually expect these promotions. This is why it is critical to offer this promotional strategy but plan it in the most profitable, strategic, and intelligent way, which can be done by leveraging analytics.

Buyers and planners along with management typically determine the merchandise levels that a promotion will be planned at to ensure the alignment of visions and strategy across areas. These levels include deciding whether the plan will be to promote total categories, such as all dresses, specific brands or collections, and specific style-colors and items. Once the level at which the promotions will be planned is determined, analysis of performance of these levels to the assortment plan is leveraged to determine the appropriate categories or items to promote. Analytical pricing software solutions enable this analysis to be performed efficiently and effectively. Historically, this was done through manual review of reports or use of reporting tools.

Once we have our customer segments and location clusters, we can leverage analytics to understand, within each cluster and customer segment, how different factors affect product demand in order to optimize the promotional strategy to drive through inventory and meet gross margin objects. Recall from our previous discussions on regular price optimization, the more sales demand, the better! Therefore, we can leverage analytical hierarchies to calculate the effects and factors and forecast demand in the future. These analytical hierarchies can leverage attributes and various hierarchical levels. Retailers can utilize this same approach to determine optimal promotions for new items that may not have historical sales.

But how do retailers know all of the item combinations that are bought together when one item is promoted? They can determine this by leveraging analytics as well. "Market basket analysis" is a term that describes looking at historical point-of-sale (POS) data by transaction to understand which items are bought together most frequently. Market basket analysis is leveraged in marketing and promotional optimization. An additional layer can be added to market basket analysis to look at what items are bought together when one item is on promotion to give insight into what items have a halo effect over others.

Cannibalism is also a factor that can be leveraged. We discussed cannibalism earlier when describing pricing analytics. In promotional optimization, cannibalism is the concept that some items may hurt the sale of other items and eat up a portion of their demand when these items are on promotion. Let's take brands as an example. Some retailers have their own brand in addition to carrying other brands. Their own brand, a private brand, is found only at this retailer and cannot be found anywhere else. Private brands also can have lower price points to drive interest and compete with national brands. However, if a national brand is on promotion, this may cannibalize the promotion of the private-label brand. The cannibalization factor can be calculated looking at how these promotions affected sales historically.

Regression analysis is leveraged to determine the effect of each factor on sales. Then time-series forecasting models are leveraged to forecast the deseasonalized data to account for trends, seasonality, and holidays. The regression component and time-series component are determined separately from each other and then combined for a final result of forecasted sales demand that takes into account trends, seasonality, promotions, and additional factors to determine the optimal promotional strategy.

"Optimization" is a term used to describe analytics that calculate and determine the ideal scenario to meet a specific target. Optimization procedures analyze each scenario and supply a score. An optimization analysis can run through hundreds, even thousands, of scenarios and rank each one based on a target that needs to be achieved. Therefore, retailers can leverage optimization to determine the ideal product and promotion, taking into account the type or promotion, such as a percentage or dollar discount, a buy one get one free, gift with purchase, as well as flyers. This optimization can also use multiobjective pricing strategies, which enable the target to be more than one specific goal.

For example, say an item is being promoted because the retailer has excess inventory and would like to increase the inventory sell through; at the same time, the retailer would like to meet the gross margin objectives of its financial plan. This would be considered two objectives. Some analytical software solutions can determine only one target. Others enable users to meet multiple targets and weight the importance of each target. So in this case, the retailer may weigh the goal of meeting the gross margin plan as 60% of the objective and selling through the inventory as 40%.

Retailers can also constrain outcomes by business rules. Certain vendors have restrictions on promotional activities. Business rules can be leveraged to ensure that these type of restrictions are being taken into account. For example, if a category of merchandise is being promoted but this category includes a national brand that does not allow promotions, these items cannot be promoted. This fact must be accounted for when viewing the final prediction of category performance based on the optimization.

Promotion optimization can also be leveraged to determine the optimal products and promotional pricing for flyers and direct mailers. Flyers are typically offered in-store as well as in newspapers. A direct mailer is a marketing vehicle that is basically a multipage flyer that is mailed to customers' homes. We will discuss marketing vehicles in more detail in Chapter 6 on marketing, but the content of these flyers and the pricing can be optimized through promotion optimization as well. The flyer's overall message and theme is generally determined by marketing and the merchandising team. For example, the general theme (the campaign theme) may be Mother's Day or spring. Analytical optimization can then determine the items within these categories that should be pictured and what the optimal promotion should be. These decisions can be determined based on driving profitability and selling through inventory.

In regard to promotional planning, many retailers leverage historical POS data that typically is stored by transaction date. This data may be stored daily. In some cases, there may be a lag of a day or even a week to when this data is available. When we think about pricing and promotional optimization in the future, the data that is leveraged will move toward real-time data. Real-time data will help retailers determine the most optimal promotion by customer. "Real-time data" refers to the availability of data as soon as that data is collected. For example, as soon as a customer removes an item from the shopping cart on a website, this data can be leveraged to determine a future action (such as 10% off on the entire purchase order). Another example of using real-time data is leveraging competitor data, such as Amazon. As soon as Amazon drops its prices on key items known to be highly price sensitive, retailers can leverage this information to drop their prices. Other industries, such as the hotel industry, have already moved to this concept. Retail is not far behind.

Leveraging real-time data would enable retailers to offer optimal promotions to customers based on their current shopping behavior on a website. In another example, say a customer places a pair of men's khaki shorts (style A) in the shopping cart but then removes that particular brand of khaki shorts from their cart for a different brand but very similar style B of khaki short. However, style A happens to be an item that the retailer has excess stock of on hand, and the item is underperforming to plan.

"Event-stream processing" is a term that describes taking specific actions or events in real time and processing these to supply an outcome. To enable personalized pricing, retailers can stream real-time data to understand customer shopping behavior and additional effects on pricing to process an optimization and deliver an output of a promotion. The retailer in this situation would be able to detect the switch of items within the basket and then, in real time, display an offer for an additional promotional discount on style A. The customer is more than likely to purchase the first style with this additional promotional offer or could potentially even buy both items.

Within the e-commerce and in-store channels, analytics has enabled the ability to personalize pricing. Price sensitivity can be determined for products at the total chain, by location, as well as by customer. Customers who shop retailers' websites provide a wealth of information to the retailers. Each time a customer logs in to the site, the retailer records movement throughout the site and the customer's behavior. Retailers now have access to information on how customers get to a website. Did they make it to the site through a Google Search, a Twitter campaign, an e-mail, or by typing in the address? Purchasing history, including pricing, is also stored at customer level. Therefore, pricing can be personalized to customers' online behavior and by leveraging competitor information in real time to make dynamic price changes.

Personalized pricing is definitely in the future for e-commerce pricing strategies. Leveraging the ability to utilize analytics and real-time data and event-stream processing would enable retailers to significantly increase profitability and inventory productivity. This approach also creates great customer experiences. Imagine if a sales associate followed you around a store and made recommendations and offered promotions as you picked up merchandise and placed it in your shopping cart. Sounds phenomenal, right? At this time, this approach is not practical for a large department store with hundreds of people walking in and out daily.

However, technology and analytics enable this type of process online. We may even see this approach in-store as technology evolves and digital carts become a reality. I can even see the possibility of having an in-store shopping model using an app. As you browse through the store, you simply scan the items that you would like to add to your cart. This real-time event-stream processing and personalized pricing could offer promotions as you shop. When you are done shopping and check out via mobile pay or your account information linked to your app sign-in, your items are ready for you to pick up at the door. We are not far off from this type of pricing model in both large-scale stores and smaller retail locations.

MARKDOWN/CLEARANCE PRICING

As merchandise begins to age, there comes a point in the product life cycle where this inventory shifts from regular/promotional pricing to markdowns (or clearance). The typical fashion product has a life cycle of 8 to 12 weeks. Once this time period has elapsed, the inventory is marked down. Seasonal products, such as coats and holiday merchandise, are also marked down at the end of the season.

I always admire the people who stock up on Christmas merchandise right after the holiday when it is marked down. I never buy something that I am going to stick in my closet and wait a whole year to use, mainly because I move too often and fear becoming a hoarder. It may also be because my birthday is after Christmas, and I spend the time buying myself birthday clothes and planning parties.

But anyway . . . The movement of merchandise to clearance generally has been based on a product life cycle timing and to clearance at a total chain level. This means that items being moved or reduced to clearance are marked down in all stores and on the retailer's website. Once it is determined that the items should be marked down, retailers leverage a markdown cadence, which refers to the determination of the schedule and price point of the initial clearance price as well as any additional price reductions. This cadence varies by retailer. Some use the same cadence across all products; others leverage a different markdown cadence by category. The initial markdown is also a component that may remain the same across the company.

So, for example, a retailer may determine that a product life cycle is eight weeks for a fashion item. After the item is in store for eight weeks, it is marked down to clearance, which for this retailer is 50% off the regular or ticket price. Two weeks after the initial markdown, the item is then reduced further to 60% off. After two weeks of being at 60% percent off, the item is reduced to 70% off. Two weeks later, the item is marked down to 80% off. In this example, the retailer is leveraging a markdown cadence across all fashion products with a four-cycle cadence: initial markdown of 50% off and subsequent cycles reducing in 10%-off increments.

Once all of the markdown cadences for an item have been exhausted, the product may be marked out of stock. At this point, the price for the product has been reduced so drastically that the retailer is losing money selling it. The selling price is actually lower than what the retailer paid for the item. Retailers try their hardest to avoid losing money. Some retailers actually donate items to charity once they have reached this point in the product life cycle. An item may end up at this particular point for many reasons. Perhaps the pricing strategy across the life cycle was not planned properly. This can occur if a retailer does not react quickly to underperformance. This could also be emotional decision making from the merchant who is reluctant to promote or to promote at too low a price. Often scenario analysis can show buyers what the repercussions of not promoting or marking an item down will be; this can lead to a stronger initial planning strategy than reacting at the point of markdown.

Let's take jackets as an example. If a specific style of jacket is not performing as expected, starting the promotional activity early on in the season can avoid markdown or clearance issues. If this item is not promoted, retailers may miss an opportunity to sell it when there is a market for jackets. Reducing the price to 50% off may drive unit sales. If this promotion does not occur, a retailer may end up with 500 units of this jacket. Before you know it, it is summertime and no one is buying jackets, even at low clearance prices. That is why it is critical to think of price planning as an overall product life cycle strategy, not a reactive approach.

Localized markdowns are another critical aspect and opportunity for retailers. Today, as mentioned, many retailers take markdowns at a chain level. Each store and the website have the same clearance items and price. If we use our jacket as an example, the item is marked down to clearance at the same time in Boston as it is in Florida. The winter season is Florida is very short, perhaps four weeks. The winter season in Boston is much more intense and lasts much longer. On the flip side, think of swimwear. Swimwear may be marked down in Boston during September, but it has a much longer life in Florida. Retail locations have varying seasonality and demand as well as varying amounts of inventory on hand even within the same region. Leveraging analytics into the assortment management process, from assortment planning, size optimization, allocation, and online order fulfillment, to promotional optimization, helps reduce unproductive inventory at the end of the season. Yet there will always be some inventory left at the end of a season.

Often clearance is important for a retailer's business model. Clearance racks and sections drive traffic into a store. Many customers only shop clearance. These customers are true bargain hunters. The concept of avoiding all clearance may not be the optimal solution for a retailer. However, those bargain hunters may be just as likely to buy the product at 30% off as at 50% off.

Analytics can enable retailers to move toward more proactive markdown optimization strategies than reactive ones and can leverage proactive promotional strategic management. As retailers are trying to offset the increased costs of shipping due to the omnichannel strategies, driving incremental revenue has become critical. Analytics can be leveraged to determine the optimal markdown cadence and the structure of the markdowns at much lower levels of the merchandise hierarchy. In the example of a retailer leveraging a markdown cadence of four cycles with the initial markdown being 50% for all products, this retailer may be losing a lot of money.

Analytical techniques can determine what the optimal percentage off should be. Instead of 50%, it may actually need to be only 30% or 40% based on the promotional offer lift, price elasticity, demand forecast, and optimization of these different scenarios. Also, based on this analytical approach, instead of having four additional markdowns, a product or product category may really require only two markdowns. Reducing the number of times the item is marked down may also be useful if the appropriate promotional activity is planned prior to clearance.

Many factors affect sales, and manually determining the optimal strategy at a local level is daunting. Leveraging analytical hierarchies for merchandise and location enables the utilization of an aggregation of data. "Aggregation" is a term that describes the sum or collection of data. Localized markdowns often can be determined by clustering locations based on climate. An added secondary component can be the price sensitivity or elasticity of stores within a climate. Localized, optimized markdown strategies are key to retailers moving forward, keeping up with the competition and driving incremental margins.

PRICING MATURITY AND ORGANIZATIONAL STRUCTURES

The analytical maturity of retailers in regard to regular, promotion, and markdown pricing differs greatly. The process, roles, and responsibilities vary. The least mature retailers typically have their merchants determining all pricing decisions based on the cost of the item as well as last year's pricing for the time frame being considered. This approach to pricing structure does not leverage localization, customer-level data, or analytical optimization.

Retailers at the next level of maturity typically have an analyst involved in the process. The analyst, who has a background in analytics, can give insight into what items may have low elasticity and can test and measure small price variations. This analyst may also give insight into what promotions are the most effective. He or she may be a member of a retailer's analytical center of excellence, which are definitely on the rise. These centers of excellence are comprised of a group of individuals who are skilled in analytics and can aid in leveraging analytics throughout different areas of the retailer.

The third level of maturity is a retailer that has pricing software solutions that enable the end merchant or planner to automate pricing decisions leveraging analytics. These pricing decisions are across the product life cycle, from regular price through to promotional pricing and markdown pricing strategies. The analytical software can also enable the retailer to localize these pricing decisions, mainly for markdown localization.

The fourth level of maturity is a retailer that has a pricing team and/or an analytical center of excellence that leverages pricing software solutions or has a built process. These retailers leverage analytical software tools to determine the optimal price. (The difference between a solution and a tool is that typically a solution is built as a click-through business process where buyers, planners, or individuals who may not be skilled in analytics can leverage the solution to create an analytically based strategy. A tool is often the core analytical capability that requires users who have been trained and educated in analytics.) This type of talent is hard to find in the retail industry. These individuals must also collaborate with the business to support day-to-day activities.

At this time, few retailers have strong product life cycle pricing optimization processes that span localization within the stores as well as personalized pricing online. This strategy will continue to evolve and increase in the marketplace as retailers continue to leverage price as a tool in their toolbox to connect to customers on an emotional level and offset increasing economic and omnichannel pressures.

Retailers must leverage analytics to plan the entire life cycle, including promotional activities and the initial clearance markdown percentage and actual cadences, to move forward and really change the game. The same type of analytical approach described for promotional optimization can be leveraged for markdown optimization. Understanding the key components of price elasticity, the marketing vehicle effectiveness, cannibalism, halo effects, and the effect of overall store-level promotions enables retailers to shape demand and plan for the future. These insights also enable retailers to optimize markdowns and drive incremental margins.

CHAPTER **6**

Marketing

magine a world where there was no such thing as junk mail. A world where every e-mail, coupon, promotional offer, or even commercial was actually of interest to you. You no longer needed to record your favorite shows on your DVR and to fast forward through the commercials because you are intrigued to hear about offers and what items are coming out in the near future. The coupons that are sent to you are for products that you actually use and become incentives for you to shop. The promotions you receive are for items that you buy and the types of promotions that you would typically act on. Marketing is headed here in the future. Let's all hope that this comes to be quickly because my e-mail and recycling bin are constantly full with junk offers.

Of course, today marketing is not only advertising. Advertising as a component of marketing has evolved to include flyers, newspaper ads, magazine ads, radio clips, television commercials, digital ads, and, my favorite, social media. Brands and retailers are now advertising on many types of platforms.

Marketing is the overall strategic planning, execution, and measuring of how a retailer or a brand interacts with its customers and how that brand is perceived. Public relations and community involvement intersect with and aid in brand perception. Marketing has become a lifetime relationship between a brand and a customer, which is why it is so critical for personalization. Customers are constantly giving retailers and brands specific information about what products they like and what promotions drive them to purchase. Just as retailers and brands expect customers to be in a lifetime relationship, customers expect that retailers and brands will listen to and leverage this information to treat them on a personal level.

DATA

The fundamental step in creating an omnichannel marketing strategy and personalizing communication with customers to grow this relationship is through joining data. The idea of understanding and knowing your customer to better communicate and drive purchases is referred to as customer intelligence. By collecting this intelligence through data, retailers can best understand customers and, in return, personalize and grow the relationship. According to a 2015 IDC study, customers who shop across more than one channel typically have a 30% higher lifetime value to a retailer. The data must be collected across all channels to truly understand the entire picture of the customer. There are a couple of ways in which retailers can collect data about their customers.

Retailers also leverage customer relationship management (CRM) solutions. A CRM solution enables retailers to store data about their customers. However, this data typically is static, such as customer records and transactional sales history, such as each time the customer made a purchase whether in-store or online, what items were purchased, and at what price point. Other interactions between retailer and customer may be logged as well, such as calls to the call center. The difference between CRM and customer intelligence is that customer intelligence leverages all data, including real-time data. "Real-time data" is a term that refers to the availability of data as soon as that data is collected. It is used to create one unified view of the customer and performs analytics on this data to gain insights in order to react and engage quickly with the customer.

One way to collect customer-level data is to create a customer loyalty program. Customer loyalty programs are rewards programs that retailers offer to customers that may offer special promotions, sneak peeks at new products, and even points or cash back on purchases to incentivize customers to shop more frequently. I personally am a huge fan of points. I travel for work so I am obsessed with collecting hotel points and Skymiles. I also shop at Walgreens because of its customer loyalty program and the coupons offered at checkout. The coupons almost always are related to items I actually buy. This is a concept called relevancy. Understanding the most relevant items, promotional types, or marketing vehicles and the most relevant communication type that drive a customer's likelihood to respond is a critical component to effective marketing.

When customers sign up for these loyalty programs, they typically give retailers their e-mail address and possibly their name, address, gender, and age. Customers are then assigned a customer loyalty ID. Through this information, retailers gain insight into customers who are signing up, such as the average age, locations, and genders, and they can also associate all of a specific customer's purchases with the customer ID. Each time a customer makes a purchase in-store, he or she gives a telephone number or e-mail address or swipes a rewards card at checkout; this associates the customer ID with the purchase. For purchases made on a website or mobile app, customer IDs typically are associated with login account information.

Customer loyalty data generally is stored in a database. Retailers typically store transaction-level data as well. A "transaction" is each individual purchase. Each time customers swipe their card, shell out cash, or press the purchase confirmation button online, a transaction takes place.

This information enables retailers to understand who their loyalty program customers are as well as what items they typically purchase, how often they visit the store, at which store they most frequently shop, and how often they purchase items online. If a customer has not opted in to a customer loyalty program, some retailers associate an ID to the credit or debit card used to pay for the transaction. This data is anonymous, but retailers can still gain insight into how frequently that card is used in the stores, what items are purchased, and where the purchase is made.

The concept of leveraging customer loyalty data to understand customer preferences and reactions to marketing campaigns was one of the first steps toward personalization. However, as the Internet has evolved, technology and capabilities have expanded the amount of information retailers can gain from their customers. The data that can be collected from the Internet and mobile data might surprise you.

Have you ever started a Google Search or cruised through your Facebook newsfeed and noticed ads for items that you were looking at the day before? These items almost haunt you till you finally give in and purchase them. Or even worse, you've already bought the items but they just keep appearing. It might feel a bit Big Brother from George Orwell's classic novel *1984*. This, in fact, is a form of advertising known as retargeting. Retargeting using web profiling tracks a user's online activity through cookies. Cookies are usually simple JavaScript files that store your browsing behavior and track your movement on websites into your browser directory. The information is usually anonymous but not necessarily.

Nonetheless, the information can be collected and used by advertisers who buy this information and advertising spots to create a profile based on your activity. They then directly target advertisements to you based on what items or types of items you have browsed. If this totally freaks you out, you can always disable your cookies in your Internet settings. You also can clean your cookie cache, which in essence cleans out your history.

This type of targeted advertising, also referred to as contextual marketing, has been used by retailers for years. However, there are a lot of issues with this approach. The first issue is that individuals may disable cookies or clean their cookie caches. Cookies also are browser specific; if an individual is on a website on Chrome but then switches to Internet Explorer, the browsing history is stored individually. With mobile devices, cookies may be automatically cleared after each Internet session, which makes it nearly impossible to store enough browsing history to make an impactful, targeted ad. Last, because this information is usually anonymous, retailers are not seeing the bigger picture of their customers. Retailers might only be annoying customers with these ads.

In addition to cookies, marketers have historically tried to leverage Internet protocol (IP) addresses to target customers. Each device that you use to surf the Internet has an associated device-specific IP address, a set of unique numbers that represent the device. If you go to Google and search "IP address," Google will display your specific IP address at the top of the results page. A device ID is a unique sequence of numbers and letters associated with each device and stays constant for the life of the product unless a factory reboot is performed. For example, Apple products have 40-digit ID numbers, which users can access through iTunes.

The IP address can indicate the location of the computer or device being used. This location service is not always accurate, and typically a third party is needed to associate the IP address with a location where the Internet service is registered. Retailers can also associate customer IP addresses with shopping behaviors. Retailers have the ability to track information from customer behavior. If a customer has created an account on a retailer's website, then when the customer logs in to his or her account, the retailer can tie the IP address to a customer ID.

If a customer uses multiple devices, such as a laptop, tablet or iPad, cell phone, and Apple Watch, and signs in on each one, the retailer can even associate all the unique IP addresses with the customer ID. Even if a person does not sign up for a loyalty program, customers who purchase an item online must give their shipping and billing addresses.

There are issues with using IP addresses just as there are with leveraging cookies. The IP address is tied to a device and an Internet service provider (ISP). Therefore, this IP address can change based on the ISP that you are using to connect to the Internet at that moment. For example, if you have AT&T cell phone service but Verizon FIOS Wi-Fi in your home, when you connect to your Wi-Fi, your IP address will change. If you were to Google "IP address" using your cell phone data, Google will display the specific device and ISP IP address. If you then connect to Wi-Fi, this IP address would change to reflect the device and new ISP. This occurs because an IP address is a set of rules or protocols used prior to and during an interaction with the Internet; the address changes as the ISP changes.

Once again, these address changes make it much harder for marketers to see clear pictures of their customers. Marketers are now moving toward leveraging device IDs to associate browsing behavior, shopping patterns, and preferences to specific customers.

There are two different approaches to cross-identifying customers with device IDs, probabilistic and deterministic. A deterministic approach occurs when a marketer associates a device ID to a customer once the customer specifically logs in to their account on the retailer's site from the device. This deterministic approach is much more accurate and widely used than the probabilistic approach, which leverages analytical models to predict and associate a customer to a specific device ID.

For example, let's say that Customer A has logged in to a Wi-Fi connection from a laptop and signed in to an account on a retailer's site multiple times. We can use a deterministic approach to say that the specific Customer A is associated with the device ID. Then the customer uses that same Wi-Fi but on their mobile device to browse the site but does not sign in to an account. This customer has browsed on the mobile device and Wi-Fi numerous times. We can use predictive analytics to determine that the same Wi-Fi connection has been leveraged numerous times. Therefore, this customer is probably Customer

A. Then we can associate the device ID of the laptop and the device ID of the mobile device with Customer A to tie together additional data. Of course, errors are possible and can be difficult to predict, so most retailers rely on deterministic approaches.

Information can be collected, stored, and structured without a device ID. Once a device ID is associated with a customer, information can be stored for the customer. This information can include how the customer got to the website. Was it through a Google Search, an ad campaign on social media, an e-mail offer, or directly to a site? Information related to how long a customer spends on each page, which items are clicked, which items are placed in the cart or basket, and the path at which the customer finally made or abandoned a purchase can be captured.

Once retailers have data related to your demographic information from signing up for the customer loyalty program, they can collect transaction data related to your shopping patterns in-store from your loyalty ID or debit or credit card number. Retailers also collect data regarding your online behavior and shopping preferences from your device IDs for each mobile device as well as from your social media behavior. This massive amount of data is collected in many different ways and channels.

According to IDC's "Key Success Factors for Digital Transformation," the largest challenge for retailers is combining information across channels. Retailers have begun to create omnichannel marketing strategies. The move from being product centric to customer centric is now viewed as critical to supporting omnichannel efforts. The customer-centric business model looks to the customer for signals in demand. It looks at what the customer is responding to from a merchandising perspective, what offers and promotions the customer is likely to respond to as well as the communication method that resonates with each individual customer—whether that is e-mail, text, or mail, for example. A customer-centric business model is different from the historical approach of being product centric, which focuses on the products the retailer wants to bring to the market regardless of customer insights.

Today we have moved from understanding only customer loyalty members to creating a 360-degree view of who the customer loyalty members are as well as customers who engage with the retailer on the website, what they buy, how they buy it, and what marketing campaigns convert them to purchase. But before we can create this 360-degree view, we have to tie this data together. With the potential of millions of customers and touchpoints, it becomes much more complex than a simple V-lookup in Excel. We are talking big data, possibly stored across multiple databases.

This is where data management becomes a critical component. Using data management techniques, we can join these data components together. We can leverage data quality techniques to standardize this data as well. For example, if customers signed up for the customer loyalty program via a pamphlet they filled out and the information then was entered into the system by an in-stores sales associate, the quality of data may be an issue. Names and abbreviations may not have been standardized. For example, different state designations may have been used, such as FL, Fla, Florida, and F. We can use text analytics to standardize this data and replace the different variations with one form of Florida. The standardization of data can be leveraged for each aspect of information, including name, device ID, address, and so forth.

Once we have this data joined and standardized, we have 360 degrees of intelligence about our customers that we can leverage to better communicate with them and continue to grow this lifetime relationship. Each communication with a customer costs retailers money. Retailers are much more likely to drive sales from current customers than to obtain new customers. Therefore, leveraging customer intelligence to make the most strategic communications with current customers will enable retailers to generate a larger return on marketing investment. According to "Omni-Channel Retail—A Deloitte Point of View," creating an omnichannel marketing initiative reduces marketing costs by more than 75%. This savings enables retailers to drive profitability, which is the key mission for any chief marketing officer.

MARKETING CAMPAIGN LIFT ANALYSIS

Historically, a "marketing event" may have been the offer of a coupon for a select time period. The lift in sales would be analyzed and compared to the cost of the event. Now that there are so many more channels by which retailers can market to and communicate with customers, it becomes increasingly important to have more advanced techniques to understand the return on the marketing campaign investment. A marketing campaign is any activity that promotes the brand or retailer. This can be in the form of a flyer that is mailed to customers, also referred to as direct mail. It can also be television or radio advertisements, investment in cookie profiling, promotional e-mails, text messages, app offers, coupons, customer loyalty offers, points, and many more kinds of promotions. Analyzing sales lifts is difficult to do manually if multiple events are going on and if different marketing campaigns are being leveraged for different customers.

Analytics are leveraged by retailers' marketing departments to determine the actual impact of each marketing campaign. Understanding the impact the marketing campaign had on the customer's purchasing decision is essential to determining the actual lift and return on investment of the marketing campaign. This is known as incremental response modeling or net lift modeling. This type of statistical modeling typically determines four segments of individuals: customers who purchase items no matter if they are offered the promotion or not, customers who purchase items only when engaged and offered a promotion, customers who are less likely to be swayed to purchase if engaged, and customers who do not respond regardless of being engaged or not. Incremental response modeling enables retailers to calculate the actual incremental benefit of the marketing campaign without blurring the lines of customers who would have bought the items regardless of the marketing campaign.

Marketing mix modeling is a statistical approach that gives insight to retailers on which marketing campaigns and mix of campaigns they should be planning. Marketers continue to ask themselves what they should be investing in and what will drive the value. Should they invest in a direct mail campaign? Should they invest in a television ad or radio clip? Should they invest in a coupon promotional percentage off discount or a coupon with $10 off the purchase of $25 or more? There are so many options for a retailer that coming up with the appropriate mix becomes incredibly difficult.

Marketing mix modeling that leverages regression analysis along with optimization to determine the most effective mix of marketing strategies attempts to achieve a target, such as sales and revenue. Regression analysis is a statistical modeling process that estimates variable relationships and helps investigate the effects of certain factors on a target. In the example of marketing mix modeling, the variables are the different marketing campaigns and the target is the additional top-line sales or revenue for the retailer. As mentioned earlier, optimization procedures analyze each scenario or possible mixture of campaigns and generate a score of the outcome. An optimization analytic can run through hundreds, even thousands of marketing campaign combinations, and rank each one based on predicted top-line sales or revenue that it will generate. Typically retailers are looking for revenue, but occasionally they will create campaigns to increase market share.

Once retailers have determined the most appropriate combination of marketing campaigns, they can plan how best to strategically engage with customers and leverage the marketing campaigns.

CUSTOMER LIFETIME VALUE

Not all customers are treated equally when it comes to marketing. Each radio slot, television commercial, social media campaign, e-mail offer, and promotional event costs the retailer money. Retailers' main goal is to drive the largest return they can on these investments. Historically, these types of offers and marketing campaigns would have been sent out to any and all customers, even if the promotion had nothing to do with items that customers were interested in. Men would get promotional offers for women's underwear. A customer who shops a retailer once a year and a customer who shops the retailer every week, no matter what the promotions are, would each get the same promotions and offers. As data has become available, technology has advanced, and analytical capabilities are leveraged, retailers can become much more strategic in an effort to increase the return on investment.

This is where the idea of customer lifetime value (LTV) is developed. Customer LTV is a predicted measurement of how much profit a retailer will retain over the lifetime relationship with a specific customer. The exact way that the customer LTV is determined may vary across retailers. The true lifetime value of a customer requires a large amount of customer-level insight over time. There are four stages of the customer relationship: acquisition, growth and loyalty, retention, and reactivity. Acquisition is the first phase of acquiring a new customer. Once the individual has become a customer, the growth and loyalty phase consists of growing the business and loyalty of the customer to the specific brand or retailer. Retention is the stage of retaining the customer through enhanced customer experience and providing the customer with relevant information, offers, communication, and merchandise to drive the customer's interest. Reactivity is the stage of reacting to a customer's decline or increase in activity through relevant communication and messages. This is done through ensuring relevancy, which is a key component of the four stages. Relevancy ensures that the customer receives the most relevant communication and promotions based on what the customer has shown interest in from their online behavior, including click-through path as well as purchase history and even social media aspects, such as likes on Instagram or retweets on Twitter.

Retailers also utilize a recency, frequency, and monetary (RFM) model to understand which customers are currently very active. "Recency" refers to how recently customers made purchases. "Frequency" refers to how regularly customers make purchases at the retailer. "Monetary" refers to the profitability associated with each customer over time. RFM models give retailers insight into their most valuable customers. It is important to ensure that the data leveraged in this model is across all channels so that retailers have a clear view of customers' value. The customer can then be prioritized and targeted depending on where they are in the customer life cycle.

We can also leverage additional elements, such as churn, or the likelihood that we will lose a customer over time. As described, understanding how to acquire customers during the acquisition phase, how to grow their loyalty over time, and then the next phase of retention to maintain their loyalty drives long-term sales. Retention is the ability to retain customers over time. Certain factors can help to predict the probability of retaining customers, such as demographics, age, competitor information, and products purchased. For example, if customers are only buying diapers from a retailer, then there is a high probability that they are purchasing these items for their children, who will eventually grow out of diapers, and the retailer may possibly lose these customers. Logistic regression is a form of regression analysis where the dependent variable is a category rather than a continuous variable. An example of a continuous variable is sales or profit. In this case, regression analysis would calculate the effects of the variables such as age, demographics, products purchased, and competitor information on the two categories: retaining the customer and losing the customer.

Retailers are able to leverage analytics to be proactive and understand which customers are likely to leave and which customers are likely to stay. Once a retailer knows the likelihood of a customer leaving, they can do two things with this information: narrow the customer's LTV or expand the customer's LTV. The retailer can narrow who truly is going to be in it for the long haul and what is the value the retailer will achieve from this customer. The most valuable customers are the key drivers to marketing spend. When retailers are able to narrow the focus to the most valuable customers, they are able to spend their marketing dollars on the most effective strategy. Or the retailer can become more proactive in engaging with this group of customers to compel them to stay. In the example of buying diapers, the retailer can offer incentives for children's clothing and other related items to lengthen the relationship.

This is an example of leveraging analytics to model and predict LTV for each customer. This measurement is often leveraged to understand who the most valuable customers are in an effort to become more strategic with marketing efforts. The higher a customer's LTV, the more the retailer may choose to invest in growing the relationship.

CUSTOMER SEGMENTATION

Because a retailer's customer population may vary from thousands to millions of individuals, personalizing marketing efforts down to a specific individual may be nearly impossible. Retailers look to analytics to aid in these efforts. Recall from Chapter 3 that, depending on the number of stores, creating different assortments for all stores becomes inefficient and close to impossible. Leveraging clusters of stores that have similar selling patterns enables efficient localization. Just as we can cluster stores based on similar selling patterns to leverage in assortment planning, we can cluster similar customers.

Customer segmentation is the first step retailers take to get to a more personalized level efficiently. Based on similar shopping preferences, customers can be clustered in two different segments in an effort to understand what products should be targeted to them. For example, if a single guy in college shops on a retailer's website and only buys men's apparel, it would make no sense to send him a flyer in the mail for baby items. This would be a complete waste of money for the retailer.

Customer segmentation is also used to understand which marketing vehicles should be leveraged for customers. For example, I never remember to bring a paper coupon so retailers should definitely not waste any money sending me direct mailers or flyers. They always end up in my recycling bin. However, I will use coupons that I receive in my e-mail. I share a similar profile to other customers; therefore, we can be grouped together to make the process more automated and efficient.

Customers can also be segmented together based on their customer LTV. This way, marketers are able to target their most valuable customers as well as those who are predicted to leave a retailer. When all of these factors are combined, advanced models can be leveraged to strategically target customers based on their merchandise preferences, the marketing vehicles that most influence them and drive them to purchase, and the value of those customers.

If retailers do not know much about a new customer, they can leverage analytics to understand the customer's initial behavior and predict the likelihood that this customer will fall into a specific customer segment. One way retailers learn more about customers and how best to segment them is through A/B testing on the web or a mobile site. Content is displayed as a form of a promotional offer or a featured merchandise category, and customer clicks on the content are tracked. Statistics related to the customers who click on the content are gathered from known customers and new ones to determine the likelihood that a new customer will fall into a certain segment. For example, say a promotional offer on the homepage promotes an additional 20% off clearance; a second offer shows a designer's new collection. Customers who click the 20% off clearance on their first trip to the site indicate that they will most likely fall into a segment that represents customers who are most likely to gravitate toward promotional offers.

Because there may be a multitude of segments, it is important for retailers to have a way to automate this process and repeat it in the future. This method is known as marketing automation. Marketing automation can be used for marketing efforts that occur on a calendar schedule, such as sending out a promotional e-mail during various times during a calendar week. It also can occur in real time and be based on customer actions or events during their path to purchase.

THE INTERNET OF THINGS

The Internet of Things, or IoT, is on the rise for retail. IoT describes the connectivity of objects to the Internet and the ability for these objects to send and receive data from each other. IoT is definitely shaping the future of all industries, including retail, health and life sciences, education, and many more. In health and life sciences, medication bottles will be leveraging IoT technology to send updates to your doctor when you are not taking your medication as prescribed. Pacemakers and other key medical devices will be able to send alerts and identify risk much quicker. IoT is impacting all industries, including retail.

Not only are these advances in technology increasing retail sales, they are changing the ways we engage with customers. Proximity marketing is a new technique that utilizes IoT technology to deliver marketing and engage with customers. A mobile device is an IoT object; when the object is near an IoT signaling device, a signal is delivered. This marketing can be in the form of local advertisements as well as direct messages. The check-in feature on Facebook is also a form of proximity marketing. If you're a millennial, I am sure you have used a filter on Snapchat that shows a cool picture of your city or state. Proximity marketing is also becoming popular. Retailers are leveraging proximity marketing on their mobile apps to send coupons, promotions, or other marketing vehicles to customers in the area of a local store in an effort to drive their path to purchase.

For example, say a retailer knows, from the online behavior, that a customer is interested in bar stools. The customer did not end up purchasing any items on the website. Now she is driving through the area and is near the local store. This retailer can now send this customer an app notification for a 20% off coupon on bar stools. This entices the customer to make a trip in the store, further accelerating her path to purchase.

Beacon technology is also a form of IoT. Beacon technology consists of small chips that utilize Bluetooth low-energy signals to communicate with other devices. Apple has created iBeacons to work on its IOS platform; they enable Apple devices to communicate with each other and send alerts and messages. Retailers are now leveraging this technology for marketing. Once customers sign in to a retailer's Wi-Fi, iBeacons enable the retailer to track them throughout the store. The traffic pathways give retailers insight into the most frequently visited spots in the store as well as enable retailers to engage directly with customers when they are in store locations. When Wi-Fi is leveraged, retailers can even tie together who you are from your mobile app login or device ID. This type of data is real time. "Event-stream processing" describes the ability to take specific actions or events in real time and to process them to supply an outcome. When retailers leverage event-stream processing, they are streaming real-time data to understand who customers are and then determine an action based on that information. Remember, the objective of the retailer is to close the sale at each opportunity.

For example, a customer downloads an app from a retailer. These apps entice customers to download because they offer promotions as well as an easy mechanism to shop. The same customer who received the app notification for 20% off bar stools from proximity marketing decided to come into the store and has made her way to the bar stool aisle. The iBeacon technology tracks her from the bar stool aisle toward the checkout counter. The customer's decision to purchase was driven by the promotion offered through proximity marketing. The retailer is also able to leverage the customer's actual activity in-store to increase their basket or size of purchase. This event would signal an additional app notification for an additional promotion on an item that the customer consistently buys when it is promoted. Beacon technology increased the customer's basket with additional products.

Say a customer is lingering near a specific product for quite a while but has not yet purchased any items. The retailer can leverage iBeacon technology to monitor this activity and then send a promotional offer to incent the customer to purchase an item. This type of activity engages with customers on a personalized level and accelerates their path to purchase.

The world of the IoT is even expanding to wearables. "Wearables" is a term that describes clothing or wearable merchandise, such as watches, that are connected to the Internet. Athletic brands seem to be at the forefront of this concept. Sneakers are now available that monitor your running style and send alerts if you appear to be running incorrectly to help avoid injury. Professional athletes have started to leverage this capability to predict injuries on the field. These wearables can also predict wear and tear. These brands can then engage with customers to alert them that it is time to buy a new pair and can even send customers offers.

PATH TO PURCHASE

"Path to purchase" is a term that describes how customers interact with different channels to ultimately purchase items from retailers. These channels can include Google Searches, e-mail campaigns, mobile apps, websites, and ads on social media sites. Retailers can track e-mail promotions sent to customers; they can collect and leverage information about customer use of promotional links or promotion codes. Throughout customer interactions with the retailer, the retailer's main goal is to drive them to purchase. These interactions are not one-time events or for one specific channel but are across channels. These interactions must be tied and seamless to drive customers to purchase. Retailers should try to close the sale at each touchpoint, whether in-store or through mobile apps, social media, or websites.

Retailers leverage customer segments to send out marketing vehicles such as an e-mail offer or mobile app coupon or notification, or to post a social media ad. These targeted promotions are sent to customers based on how likely they are to act upon the promotion. Incremental response modeling leverages analytics to determine the likelihood that customers will respond. Specifically, this modeling enables retailers to strategically leverage promotions by understanding which customers would have made a purchase regardless of the offer. These promotions then attract customers to the website or store. Once customers have logged in to the website or enter the store, personalized content can be served up to them based on their preferences. These preferences have been collected over time as the items that customers click on and add to their basket or cart, and are analyzed.

Merchandise attributes can be leveraged for this type of analysis to show customers merchandise with similar attributes. Market basket analysis can also be leveraged to drive what customers purchase at one time. Market basket analysis is a statistical analysis that leverages historical sales to determine what items are most frequently purchased together. This could be a dress with a pair of heels or a bowtie with a sport coat. With this type of analysis, retailers can make product recommendations to customers while on the site.

Retailers can also start to leverage machine learning algorithms to learn what types of products interest customers. As described in Chapter 3, "machine learning" is enabling computer programs to learn over time as new data becomes available through artificial intelligence. This type of analytical programming can learn more about customers' online shopping behavior over time and start to predict which items customers will likely click on and purchase. Retailers are leveraging this information to personalize content on their web pages and to create personalized assortment recommendations. Offering relevant products to customers moves them one step closer to closing a deal. It also enhances the customer experience and gives customers the sense of personalization that they desire.

Personalized pricing is also another driver for the customer's path to purchase, as we described in Chapter 5. Based on customers' determined product preferences and their sensitivity to price, retailers can leverage this information to show not only personalized content but also pricing and relevant promotions. This is where retailers are able to become much more strategic in their promotions rather than giving it all away. Once retailers have a clear view of their customers through the data that has been collected and brought together, they can determine if customers will still purchase an item regardless of a promotion. This way, retailers give discounts only to those customers who need the discount to accelerate their path to purchase. The same logic applies to free shipping.

When it comes to promotional content, many retailers utilize A/B testing to help understand customers in an effort to segment them and to determine the most effective content, promotion, and placement of offers. In this type of A/B testing, two different content pages or promotions are compared to see which one has the higher performance. This could be as simple as testing whether an advertisement for a specific brand or collection should be on the left side of the page or the right side. It may also be a promotion featured on the top of the page versus the middle of the page. Retailers leverage business rules to determine content along with customer segments. Retailers can assign specific content to be displayed to customers based on the segment they are in.

If customers do not make a purchase on the website, the path does not end there. Creating a seamless path throughout each channel is critical in the evolving omnichannel world. Relevant blogs can be featured on social media to encourage customers to return. Promotional e-mails can be leveraged. As customers physically approach a location, proximity marketing can be used to remind them to visit the store. iBeacons can help drive customers to purchase in-store and send select offers through mobile apps. In-store associates can leverage information about customers to prepare them to close the sale. Customer information can be shared across the business through reporting and visualization tools to equip in-store associates with the information necessary to drive a customer's path to purchase.

At each point in the purchasing journey, retailers are seamlessly leveraging a clear understanding of who the customers are, what their shopping behavior has been, what their merchandise preferences are, how sensitive they are to price, and what promotions drive them to purchase. This data is no longer in silos. The retailers' main goal is to bring together intelligence about customers to create a relationship and further understand customers. It is all about creating a true omnichannel customer experience and driving long-term customer relationships.

Retailers have varying levels of maturity across each part of the business process. When it comes to marketing, the maturity level can be thought of as having five phases. Phase 1 consists of determining customer segments. It moves retailers from treating each person's promotions and communication the same to starting to vary the communication and promotions toward becoming more relevant. Phase 1, for example, starts to ensure that a single man in his 20s is not getting a promotional e-mail for diapers. Once retailers have better understanding of their customer segments, they can then manage their campaigns and promotions more effectively, which is phase 2. Optimization is phase 3 and moves a retailer from adding in the element of relevancy to optimizing the relevant products along with the most strategic use of marketing dollars to increase the retailer's return on investment. Understanding which customers would likely have purchased an item regardless of promotion or coupon enables retailers to increase revenue. Phase 4 consists of leveraging real-time data and advanced technology, such as the IoT, to further drive relevant communication with customers. This occurs after retailers have moved to customer segmentation, campaign management, and optimization, which are the components of phases 3 and 4. Throughout this process, the customer is always at the center. Phase 5 leverages analytical capabilities to understand the attribution and lifetime value of customers, how best to avoid churn, and how to ensure retention along with further growth and loyalty.

Each step in the right direction helps to guide retailers to a further relationship and loyalty from their customers. These strategic processes also enable retailers to drive success while improving profitability and increasing market share. As you can see, each step in the retailer's business process directly relates to the others and puts the customer at the center through the path to purchase. It takes an entire team to successfully manage a business. Without the relevant communication with customers, merchandise buying and planning teams would have a difficult time enticing customers into the stores to see the most relevant assortment offerings. At the same time, the marketing team relies on the product assortments and product pricing strategies to aid in driving customers' paths to purchase.

CHAPTER **7**

In-Store
Experience

Technology is ever evolving, and customers are able to shop any which way they choose. It is becoming more and more convenient to shop online. I have a young son and the idea of going into a store with him makes me cringe. It is always hit or miss with him. Sometimes he's a great personal shopper. His fashion icon is Chuck Bass from *Gossip Girl*, so I think he has the potential to be a very well dressed young man one day. But it can also turn into a battle with bribery being the only way to get out of the store. When I am shopping on my own, I enjoy the experience, and so do many other people. In-store shopping is transforming into in-store experiences. It is all about creating an enjoyable time for customers to take time out of their day to visit a store.

Years ago, people got style tips and ideas through trips to the mall. Today social media and fashion blogs have become outlets for individuals to express their style, share with others, and cultivate their own sense of fashion. Specialty stores and retailers are creating in-store experiences to compete with the social media world. Visual merchandising, creating a visual environment that draws customers, was the first step toward creating these in-store experiences. The idea of creating a great ambience was the beginning of creating in-store experiences.

Although social media is on the rise, customers still love to shop in actual stores. Around 10% of sales are done online on average; for millennials, that ratio rises to about 19%. We discussed the concept of showrooming in Chapter 1. This notion of leveraging brick-and-mortar locations as showrooms for customers to feel, touch, and see products in person but eventually buy online has created complexities for in-store teams.

STORE LABOR FORECASTING

Analytics can be leveraged to help solve the additional complexities of showrooming and to create impactful and intriguing in-store experiences. Labor forecasting can be incredibly challenging for a retailer. Understanding exactly how many sales associates and managers are needed by day and by hour is difficult. Many factors affect scheduling. Typically the number of hours that a store must schedule depends on the sales volume of the location and the particular time of the year.

Determining these hours has become more difficult as online sales and showrooming have increased.

Certain events also affect the traffic a store receives. A sporting event or a concert in the local area can dramatically increase traffic numbers; you can't predict these increases by looking at historical traffic and sales volume. On the flip side, traffic may decrease due to construction or a new competing store opening nearby. Statistical forecasting is an analytical tool that is leveraged for labor forecasting and scheduling. Statistical forecasting can forecast store volume as well as traffic or transactions. Some retailers use door sensors to monitor the number of customers who walk into their locations. Statistical forecasting leverages historical traffic or transactions as well as causal factors, such as in-store promotions that drive more traffic. It also can leverage periodic events, such as sporting events, craft fairs, festivals, and concerts, that may increase or reduce traffic. The forecasting capabilities can also account for the shifts in holidays, such as Black Friday and Mother's Day.

Retailers that leverage these additional factors in addition to historical patterns gain a much more accurate view of projected traffic and staff needs. This knowledge also enables retailers to understand the entire trade area demand in order to account for showrooming. An understanding of the online demand within a local store can help retailers to determine how many additional staff members are required to support showrooming customers.

ASSORTMENT OPTIMIZATION

Utilizing the ability to curate assortments and plan merchandise inventory based on trade area demand also enables analytics to drive the in-store experience. Having the right assortment for customers is essential to ensuring that their in-store experiences are successful. The assortments must also be right for customers down to the size level. Leveraging size optimization to take into account the true size demand of the store's customer base ensures that customers can come into the store to touch, feel, see, and try on the item. Having inventory visibility across channels is essential to supporting this process. Customers should be able to check online to see if a specific item is offered in their local store as well as if their size is currently available.

Optimization also enables retailers to optimize the space of the store. Downsizing is a key trend in the industry. When the economy was at an all-time high, retailers invested in real estate. Stores were bought or built and at large footprints. As we discussed, the housing market crashed in 2007. The following year, gas prices took a spike and unemployment rates rose. Consumer spending declined. It has since risen back to somewhat comparable levels prior to the housing market crash in 2007. However, in this time frame, the digital landscape evolved. Competition is high and customers are becoming much savvier in regard to comparison shopping and coupon clipping. Same-store sales year over year have declined. Customers hardly ever buy all items at one retailer.

This has caused a decline in sales per square foot at retail store locations. Sales per square foot is calculated to determine the productivity of a real estate investment. This metric simply takes the total dollar sales for a specific store on an annual basis and divides this number by the total square feet within the retail store. It can also be calculated at a lower level other than total store. For example, if the home division is featured within a specific square footage of the store, then the productivity of the home division can be calculated. This calculation would be the total annual sales of the home division divided by the associated square footage.

In-store productivity has taken a big hit since the 2007 recession. Even today, many retailers have to make tough decisions about closing stores and/or reducing store square footage. Retailers are looking to add restaurants, salons, stores within a store, and many other tactics to make up for this decline. Urban Outfitters has tested opening pizza shops within their locations to help with productivity and create that in-store experience of a laid-back environment where individuals hang out, shop, and eat. Other retailers have placed popular makeup stores or hair salons in their stores. Some retailers have looked to downsize. They often close large locations and move to smaller ones or consolidate within a given trade area. Determining which stores to close and assessing the impact of these closings is a challenge. Analytics can help users do scenario analysis, which leverages optimization to run through hundreds of scenarios and determine the optimal locations to close and the expected impact on revenue based on the forecasted future sales and revenue.

Retailers have also moved to smaller locations and have therefore had to do more with less. Earning more revenue with less square footage also requires optimization. When we think about initially curating assortments based on trade area demand, we leverage analytics to determine what that assortment should be. From there, we can further optimize this assortment down to a location perspective for hardline products, taking in to account spatial constraints. "Hardline" and "softline" are terms used in retail to describe products in two separate categories. Softlines are items that are literally soft, such as clothing. Hardlines are hard items, such as appliances and dinnerware. Hardline items typically have specific product dimensions. Analysts utilize planograms, which are diagrams that show the specific space and dimensions of the fixtures that items are merchandised on. Planograms are used to estimate how much each store can hold of these items and how much space each has from a spatial perspective. Then retailers use the information from these planograms (e.g., how many facings are available, how many shelves there are and the dimensions of shelf capacities) to determine the best possible assortment.

Customer decision tree analysis is a statistical process that analyzes merchandise attributes or characteristics to determine what really drives the customer's decisions. Let's use K-Cups as an example. I absolutely love my Keurig machine. Retailers have only a certain amount of space to dedicate to K-Cups. Customers tend to purchase based on brand as well as flavor. Retailers can leverage these attributes to determine what the optimal mix of brands and flavors should be based on available space in each store. Customers do not want to see all the flavors of Starbucks. They want to see a mix of brands, such as Dunkin' Donuts, McCafé, Green Mountain, and Starbucks.

Customers also want to see a wide assortment of flavors. How do we ensure that we have the right range of flavors and brands? We do not want to have only one brand, and we do not want to see only French Vanilla. Leveraging advanced analytical capabilities to optimize based on these customer decision tree components, product dimensions, store-level forecasted demand, and spatial constraints enables retailers to optimize assortment as well as space, which further helps them to do more with less.

Retailers also leverage higher- or macro-level space planning and optimization to determine how best to increase store space productivity. Space planning can be used to plan the space associated with divisions, categories, or subcategories to best plan inventory. Categories that mix softlines and hardlines become a bit more challenging to analyze, but it can be done if the space available for each is known. Even if retailers do not leverage space planning, they most always utilize some form of space planning when opening new stores or remodeling stores. It is essential to plan the space prior to bringing in merchandise and setting the floor from a visual merchandising perspective. Such planning also helps store planners and allocation analysts to determine how much product a store needs to support a grand opening or reopening.

THE INTERNET OF THINGS

Inventory visibility has historically been a challenging task. Typically, retailers store and update inventory on a nightly basis. Offering real-time inventory information requires additional tracking. "RFID" stands for "radio frequency identification." This type of technology can be leveraged to track inventory. RFID technology enables real-time data of inventory down to the specific stock-keeping unit (SKU) and can even aid in theft detection. This data can also be used to track inventory on its way to the retailer. Grocery stores can utilize this technology to track inventory and quality control. Ice cream is a great example of an item that is tracked for inventory as well as temperature. If the temperature of ice cream rises to a certain level, it can cause consumers to become ill.

In addition to offering customers the right assortment at the right size and visibility to inventory in local stores, analytics can be applied to make product suggestions. "Clienteling" is a term that describes the ability for store associates to use this data to help drive customers to purchase and to build stronger relationships with customers. Just as we are able to use this data to create analytical models to suggest products and offer promotions when necessary, store associates can do the same. Information related to the customers' preferences can be accessed by the associates through reports, tablets, and mobile devices.

True Religion is a clothing retailer based in California; they have given their sales associates Apple Watches to access customer information to leverage in the sales process and increase customer engagement. Also, once a customer who has registered on True Religion's app enters the store, a sales associate is notified through the Apple Watch and given that customer's preferences. True Religion is a great example of the future of leveraging customer insights in-store.

The same modeling techniques leveraged to determine product recommendations and promotions are used in-store. The only difference is that instead of the information being displayed on the webpage, analytical insights can be given through reports, tablets, or even Apple Watch notifications to store associates to offer to the client. This approach really makes customers feel that they are the center of attention; who doesn't love to feel like that? This is truly personalized service. These insights can be displayed to the store associate leveraging reports and dashboards on their tablet as well as on wearables such as smart watches. Not only does clienteling create great in-store experiences for customers, it also helps store associates to increase customers' purchases and close sales.

Units per transaction (UPT) is a key performance indicator that store staff are graded on. UPT is all about upselling customers once they are in the store. Remember the small price-point items close to the register? These items are typically categorized as impulse buys. Customers normally don't go into stores just for these items. Instead, they see these items while waiting in line and decide to purchase them on the fly, unplanned. These items, which typically are general ones, are tactically placed there to help increase the number of items customers purchase per transaction (the UPT). Retail is moving to the point where a cashier will be able to understand a customer's specific profile. Instead of the cashier or sales associate suggesting generic impulse buy items, suggesting items that a customer actually is interested in purchasing based on past history is where the additional in-store opportunity to leverage these analytical insights comes into play. Often, retailers have "add-on" sale items located close to the register in an effort to suggest these items and add them on to the sale. The suggested add-on items can be further tailored to the items that are most relevant to the customer. In boutiques where there is enough staff to cater to each customer, the suggestions can be additional items that are brought to the register as recommendations from additional associates.

iBeacon technology was described in Chapter 6 as a means for marketing and engaging with customers. Once customers sign in to a retailer's Wi-Fi, the iBeacons enable the retailer to track them throughout the store. This technology can alert store associates to customers. In a large department store during a peak time on a Saturday, it may be close to impossible to clientele all customers. However, if store associates learn that a customer with a projected high lifetime value or one who has a high likelihood of churn is in the store, associates can give these key customers their attention. Just as there is only a certain budget for marketing and retailers are looking to become as strategic as they can with their budgets, the same is true for store associates.

Retailers can use iBeacon technology to track customers' journeys throughout the store. They can analyze traffic pathways based on this data. A traffic pathway shows where most customers first walk to, what areas are most heavily visited, and areas where the traffic is relatively low. Traffic pathways give retailers insight into the most frequently visited spots in the store and enable them to directly engage with customers when they are in a store location. This type of information gives insight into where products should be placed. If a common, high-selling item, such as socks, is placed in the back of the store, customers must walk past hundreds of opportunities to find additional products to purchase on their trip.

Mobile apps will continue to grow as a part of the in-store experience. The ability to use a mobile app while in store to scan an item's barcode and find additional information is increasing. If retailers do not leverage mobile apps, they risk losing customers to competitors. Mobile apps are also great ways for retailers to track and understand what interests customers. The more ability and opportunities for retailers to engage and collect information about customers, the better. Each engagement enables the retailer to close a sale and grow the customer relationship.

This is especially useful in the fitting room, which is an extremely important part of the customer journey. Customers go to fitting rooms after a retailer has their attention and they have found a product that interests them. Mobile apps that enable customers to alert sales associates to bring additional sizes or, in one click, order a size that may not be available in the store are all about creating convenience and increasing sales. These apps can also be leveraged to track customers. Customers who check in to a fitting room and enable fitting room settings via their mobile app can receive alerts, promotions, and product recommendations. The retailer's app also alerts sales associates about specific customers who have entered the store and have a high customer lifetime value.

Retailers are also leveraging tablets and digital screens within fitting rooms for customers to request additional sizes of items. This technology can also be leveraged to offer product suggestions and promotions, just as sales associates are doing in the form of clienteling. The digital clienteling capabilities in a fitting room scale to extremely busy peak times when there just are not enough sales associates available. Specialty retailers are leveraging these devices to enable customers to cruise their assortment from a comfy seat while sipping complimentary champagne. The items are then collected by sales associates, and customers are notified when the items are ready in the fitting room.

This type of technology and approach is radically changing the in-store experience. Online retailers also are leveraging these concepts to create brick-and-mortar locations virtually. Virtual reality (VR) technology is at the forefront of these concepts as well. VR technology is a computer-simulated replication of reality. VR headsets, which are the way of the future, can simulate an actual store. Imagine being able to put on a headset and virtually walk through the endless aisles of Amazon. The term "endless aisle" is often used to describe the ability to order items at a kiosk in a retail store that may not be available or offered at that specific location. VR technology takes the concept of the endless aisle even further.

Visual analytics can be integrated into VR technology. While you are roaming through the virtually simulated store wearing virtual goggles, analytical insights about you offer promotions and direct you to locations with products that most interest you. You select products, pick them up, and place them in your virtual basket, then check out with a push of a button. The actual items are then delivered to your home in days. Sure, this concept might not go mainstream for quite some time, but select specialty retailers will hop on the bandwagon to become a futuristic e-retailer. The concept of virtual stores is truly a way of creating an experience in-store for customers as well. Imagine being able to test out how a couch will look in your own home or how a bike rides as you virtually ride it through the mountains. VR technology is a game changer for brick-and-mortar locations that look to compete with Internet shops.

VR technology also can support store visits. Corporate retail staff typically visit stores as part of the planning process to understand how the stores look from a visual perspective. Executives visit stores to talk to store management about opportunities and risks. Reports and numbers cannot supply the whole picture. Walking through a store gives executives insight into how displays look and how visual merchandising is working. Often executives engage with customers firsthand when walking through stores. This process helps to tie merchandising and the in-store experience together. Store operations typically have district managers, regional managers, and additional layers within their organizational structure on the store operations side. These layers of management visit stores as well. Buyers make store trips to see how their assortment looks on the selling floor and to understand feedback from area managers and sales associates. Planning and allocation teams visit stores to check on inventory levels.

These teams visit local stores as well as different store locations across their portfolio. Global retailers must fly internationally, which is costly, and all trips incur additional expenses. Retailers will leverage this technology in the future to walk through stores without having to leave the corporate office. Regional managers can routinely check in on stores through virtual reality technology while lowering the overall costs of operations. Buyers would be able to see how an assortment looks as soon as it arrives on the floor.

The ability to actually see analytics will merge with virtual reality technology. As buyers look at their assortment on the sales floor, analytical insights are displayed through the augmented reality goggles. Initial sell-through key performance indicators are displayed as well as future forecasted demand for a certain area. Sales in-store versus online are displayed, as is the primary customer segment that has been purchasing the item along with insight into these segments to understand who this product is resonating with and compare that to the initial assortment plan. Promotional effectiveness is shown when you turn your head to look at another category area. If you look down, it will display footsteps on a heat map. This insight is leveraged to show what the traffic is for a particular area within that store.

Of course, in-person store visits will still be required in order to connect with management and customers on a personal level. Nevertheless, leveraging augmented reality to virtually walk through stores will significantly reduce the amount of travel expenses a retailer incurs. This technology is becoming cheaper each year; today, VR goggles can be purchased for under $100 a pair.

The overall goal of leveraging analytics is to create an enjoyable, convenient, and personal experience for the customer. Leveraging statistical forecasting to predict store traffic more accurately enables retailers to better forecast store labor. A more accurate and efficient store labor schedule enables the right level of customer service; sales associates can give customers the attention, service, and personalization that they deserve. These store associates can leverage clienteling to create a personalized experience by utilizing analytical insights delivered to the associate through tablets or even smart watches. This same type of personalization, giving customers product recommendations and promotional offers where needed, can be served up through mobile apps and fitting room technology. Product visibility across channels and stores along with one-click ordering accompanied by free shipping further enhances the convenience and delivers an omnichannel experience.

Ensuring that the appropriate assortment is available for this particular customer is a critical component to an in-store experience that will drive him or her to purchase. Retailers are having to do more with less due to the popularity of digital channels and demand moving online. Assortment optimization as well as leveraging analytical optimization techniques to plan the most productive assortment within the constraints of the space is key to helping retailers be more effective.

Last, leveraging the newest technological advances in the IoT enables retailers to further personalize and engage with customers as soon as customers reach the proximity of the store location all the way through to checkout. These technological advances, including virtual and augmented reality, are shifting the way we think about the in-store experience, how retailers travel to their locations, and how the future of an endless aisle is right around the corner. Analytics not only help retailers increase their profitability but also make the in-store experience one that is inviting and entertaining for customers. The in-store experience is all about the customer experience and the growth of the customer lifetime value.

CHAPTER 8

Cybersecurity

illions of Americans work hard each day to save money in order to give their children a good life. These individuals may be counting change and working late hours and multiple jobs and getting by on minimum wage. Imagine if these hardworking individuals logged into their bank accounts one day to see them completely empty. Every single penny completely gone with absolutely no idea what happened to it. Not being able to pay their rent that is due the next day and be able to keep a roof over their heads. Not having a dime to buy food to feed their children even though they worked so hard to save.

This scenario often is the outcome of a data breach. While all Americans are subject to data breaches, lower-income families may not have multiple accounts or the funds to hold them over until the bank can credit the stolen money back. Debit card and credit card information is often stolen and made available for criminals to completely wipe out people's bank accounts. A cyberattack is when an entity's computer systems are damaged or destroyed. Most often, large, well-established banks credit funds back within 24 hours when fraudulent activity occurs. However, smaller banks may take weeks to investigate and return the money; sometimes stolen funds are never returned to victims.

Since 2011, over 236 million confidential records containing personal data have been breached. These data breaches occur across industries, not only in retail. Among healthcare organizations, 91% have experienced a data breach once in the last two years. In 2014, the federal government experienced over 61,000 cybersecurity breaches. These numbers are startling. What are these industries doing to avoid these attacks and ensure that customers' information is safe?

Cybersecurity is the ability to protect against the unauthorized use of electronic data. This electronic data can be personal customer information, such as names, addresses, social security numbers, credit cards, and debit cards, among others. Cyberattacks are on the rise. Criminals find it much easier to attack electronically rather than rob banks. In an effort to protect individuals, standards for storing and handling payment card information, also known as PCI, have been established. These standards are known as the Payment Card Information Data Security Standard (PCI DSS). Even with these standards in place, hackers still successfully seize confidential data. This costs retailers millions of dollars. These types of breaches also significantly hurt retailers' reputations, which also leads to lost sales.

Whether an attack on an individual or a large retailer, many data breaches start off with phishing techniques. "Phishing" is a term that describes when an attacker poses as someone else or an actual company to gain confidential information. One of the most popular forms of phishing is through e-mail. An attacker sends the victim an e-mail that directs him or her to a link or a download. Once the victim clicks on this link, malware is downloaded onto the computer. "Malware" is software that aims to steal information or corrupt the hardware. In this case, the malware enables the hacker to gain access to the victim's credentials. This has been going on for years. Over time, hackers have refined their techniques so that it is very hard to truly know if an e-mail or site is legit or is a phishing effort. This is why it is important to always go directly to the site by typing in the URL rather than clicking a link in an e-mail.

This type of attack started way back in the day when criminals used landlines—phones that are actually connected by metal wires or telephone connection cords. These criminals would pose as legitimate companies and ask for payment on a late bill or some other type of fraudulent request. Prior to cyberattacks, criminals would visit homes acting as emissaries for companies with unpaid bills or for charities asking for donations. Although these hackers now use modern techniques, they still aim to convince innocent people that they are someone else or a legitimate company in an effort to steal.

Criminals approach cyberattacks in many different ways, but often phishing is used. Once criminals gain an employee's credentials, they can hack into company systems. Most often once criminals have infiltrated a retailer's systems, they still are not able to access secure data. Because of PCI DSS, not every employee within a retailer can access secure data. But once criminals are in, they can create the same type of admin decoy to take down the next wall of security and obtain the secure data. Querying or searching through different databases enables hackers to see what each database contains. A database is a set of data contained in a location on a network, computer, or server. Typically, different data sets are stored in different databases. So when you think of confidential payment card information, this data is stored on a different database from, let's say, product inventory. While helping a customer, sales associates may query product inventory databases to see which local stores have a specific size of an item. These sales associates would not have access to a database with payment card information.

Employee administrative roles within organizations have much wider access. Once hackers have made their way into internal systems, they can steal an administrator's credentials and/or create an additional administrative user. Once hackers create an administrative user for themselves, they can utilize this additional authority to move one step closer to the mission. Since the hackers then can query and search which databases are available and what components make them up, they can further hone in on the target. Hackers now know which database they are targeting and have created an additional administrative user account that they can attack.

A database often contains files that are uploaded or files that have an automated upload process that occurs monthly, weekly, daily, or more frequently to support the business. Hackers take advantage of these files. Hackers have been known to replace regularly uploaded files with files containing a virus or malware. Once the file has been opened or uploaded, the malware is downloaded. The malware can give hackers the data they are targeting or insert a crippling virus that could take down a retailer's business functions.

However, this approach would not give hackers access to customer credit and debit card data because the PCI DSS requires that this sensitive data not be stored on a database that can be retrieved. Unfortunately, point-of-sale systems do contain this information. To gain access on these systems, hackers install malware onto POS systems. Once they have placed malware on the systems, they can track and store transaction history, including the credit and debit card information. Hacking a POS system typically occurs on a very large scale, with sometimes over 50 million individuals affected in one attack. Credit and debit card information of victims is compromised, and they are often victimized by theft and fraudulent purchases. Banks and credit card companies experience large financial losses from these attacks. Not only are these companies tasked with sifting through purchases to determine the fraudulent transactions, they must refund customer money and send new credit or debit cards. The organizations incur additional expenses for these efforts.

The additional expenses at banks create tension between banks and retailers. When a data breach occurs, customers feel vulnerable and taken advantage of, which can cause them to fear shopping at the retailer. This type of fear can affect overall customer lifetime value and have significant impacts on a retailer's future sales and profitability. Retailers can leverage analytics to prevent or minimize the risk of these data breaches. Most often, this type of cyberattack creates suspicious activities. The first instance of suspicious activity was the creation of an additional administrative user role. The second type of suspicious activity was the querying of database information to determine which databases contained the information hackers were targeting.

Suspicious activity such as user creation or abnormal querying of databases is stored and can be graphed and visualized. Once this activity is visualized, suspicious spikes in activity that can indicate threat of an attack can be identified. Cybersecurity teams often have a protocol to send an alert when suspicious activity occurs. However, many times these alerts are not leveraging advanced analytics, and therefore alerts become quite common. Like the boy crying wolf, it becomes increasingly difficult to determine which alerts are real and which are false alarms. Advanced statistical modeling can leverage this data to predict the likelihood that a specific activity poses a threat. For example, if a hacker created an administrative user role to leverage for additional permissions and authorization, this activity is logged. The querying of all databases can also be logged. Analytics can predict that the behavior of a new administrative user who performs certain types of querying is uncommon, and flag the activity as a threat. Machine learning algorithms can leverage a multitude of data points that are stored to learn what normal activity is and then determine when abnormal or suspicious activity occurs.

Historically, retailers do not employ such advanced analytics until they have been victims of data breaches and gone through lawsuits and reductions in sales and customer relationships. However, as data breaches increase, retailers are making this type of approach much more of a priority.

Card readers called skimmers have been used to capture and steal credit and debit card data. Criminals place these skimmers on ATMs and gas station credit card pump machines, for example, to steal credit and debit card information, much like hackers attacking POS systems but on a smaller scale. Skimmers copy the magnetic strip, which contains the account information, when victims place their cards into the card-reading devices.

EUROPAY, MASTERCARD, AND VISA/CHIP CARDS

Europay, Mastercard, and Visa (EMV) cards have been created to help combat or minimize these efforts. These newer cards have a chip that contains encrypted credit card and/or debit card information along with the customer's information. Users place their cards into the chip reader instead of swiping the magnetic strip. Each time the card is utilized in a transaction, the encrypted code changes. Chip card transactions also require personal identification numbers (PINs) or signature, which makes it very difficult for hackers to steal account and credit or debit card information to re-create cards for use in fraudulent purchases.

The United Kingdom, which has been utilizing chip cards for much longer than the United States, has seen a reduction in fraudulent purchases of over 67% since these card restrictions were implemented. The UK chip cards require PINs, not signatures, which drastically reduces the likelihood that criminals could compromise a card (a PIN is harder to replicate than forging a signature). However, EMV chip card technology used in the United States still is anticipated to reduce fraudulent activity.

CHARGEBACKS

When fraudulent purchases are made, retailers as well as victims are negatively affected. Each time a purchase is flagged as fraudulent, retailers must refund the money to victims. This refund is known as a chargeback. Retailers typically must make chargebacks when customers do not receive the product or did not make the purchase. The purchase might be flagged as fraudulent and require a chargeback *after* the goods or services have been delivered. So basically, criminals can purchase items with a stolen credit card and receive the items. Then the victim flags the item as fraudulent and requires a chargeback. The retailer must refund the money even though the item is no longer in its possession. The retailer has now basically given criminals items for free and has to pay for the loss. The retailer also has to pay a fee for each fraudulent activity to the bank or credit card company, which also negatively affects the relationship between the bank/credit card company and the retailer.

Retailers can minimize the risk of fraudulent purchases that require chargebacks. Just as suspicious activity can be flagged, so can fraudulent activity related to customer purchases. Leveraging machine learning and predictive analytics, retailers can learn which activities are considered normal for card users and which activities and purchases are predicted to be fraudulent. Fraudulent purchases can be predicted looking at different components, such as items that are most frequently fraudulent purchases, the price points that generally are fraudulent, and the location where the transactions are taking place.

DATA GOVERNANCE

An additional component to monitoring activity and predicting suspicious activity is the need for data governance. Data governance, by definition, is the security of data as well as the availability to users. Data governance ensures that employees are not able to access confidential data and data that they do not need to do their day-to-day jobs. For example, human resource data, which contains employee salaries and confidential information, must be locked down. Data governance ensures that this information is accessible only by employees who need the information and have clearance to access it. Data governance is a vital aspect of cybersecurity. If personal credit card information was accessible by any employee, the risk of a data breach and stolen customer information would be much higher, and these breaches would occur even more frequently. The risk of a breach in personal information is why the PCI DSS was developed.

Take, for example, the scenario where hackers capture an employee's credentials. If an employee had access to any and all data, the hackers would be able to steal data much more quickly. Data governance provides structure within an organization. It also ensures that employees pull the information they are looking for within a database.

Often retailers store many different key performance indicators. Sometimes this data may vary based on its aggregation or calculation level. The data can also vary on the frequency that it is updated. Data governance ensures that end users are able to access the correct data that they need to perform their job duties.

Cyberattacks and fraud have created a wealth of challenges for retailers and banks. Retailers have employed cybersecurity techniques to minimize the risk of these criminal actions in an effort to protect their customers, brands, and profitability. The customer is always the center of the retailer's priorities in all aspects of the business. Customers must feel that they can safely make purchases, whether in-store or online, without the threat of credit and debit card theft. The safety of customers' sensitive information is critical to protecting the retailer's relationship with customers and their lifetime value. This is also true for the relationship between retailers and banks and credit card companies. Leveraging machine learning techniques and predictive analytics minimizes risk by identifying threats and alerts. Machine learning and predictive analytics can also alert and predict which suspicious activities and purchases are fraudulent. This type of proactive approach reduces chargebacks for retailers. EMV chip cards and data governance are also proactive measures that are utilized to minimize risk and prevent malicious and fraudulent activities.

CHAPTER **9**

Customer Journey

The most important aspect of retail is the customer journey. The customer should be at the center of all business units and processes within a retailer's overall business process. The entire retail process of planning a strategic plan, curating assortments, fulfilling inventory, pricing, marketing, and in-store experience and cybersecurity should all be centered on customers and their journeys. The main mission of a retailer is to provide a seamless, enjoyable, and convenient shopping experience across all channels of the business. A retailer's main goal is to increase overall profitability and strategically drive a customer's path to purchase and continue to purchase items, increasing the customer's lifetime value.

The customer is truly the center of a retailer's business process. Understanding the customer's preferences, what drives a customer to purchase, what promotions incent a customer to shop, and what marketing vehicles reach a customer most effectively is the first step to becoming customer centric. The insights into a customer's preference for products help to drive the merchandise financial planning process in the beginning of the season. Understanding high-level merchandise trends based on the customer's preferences to statistically forecast strategic financial objectives at a division, department, or category level ensures that future demand is anticipated in order to plan inventory levels and inventory productivity accurately.

These strategic merchandise financial plans are then broken down to item-level plans, also known as assortment plans. Curating the assortment, which means leveraging customer insights to understand which brands, silhouettes, colors, and items will drive the business, ensures that customers will find the right products. Moving from the historical approach of merchandise-centric assortment planning to customer-centric assortment planning enables assortments to be more in line with what customers demand. Taking into account customer behavior, such as social media activity and influence, is a critical component today as the world of social media continues to evolve into customers' main points of styling ideas. As customer preferences are ever changing, leveraging predictive analytics, such as regression analysis, to predict future trends of merchandise attributes and attribute combinations gives retailers a competitive edge.

Statistical forecasting down to the item level along with new item forecasting ensures that a more accurate future demand projection is available for each item. The accuracy of sales plans is significantly increased when the statistical forecast, which leverages historical sales, trends, seasonality, holiday shifts, and causal factors such as promotions, is utilized in the planning process. The analytical approach of deriving a sales plan also creates efficiency for retailers, avoiding manual plan creation.

Advanced optimization techniques enable retailers to take into account multiple factors, such as sales, Instagram likes, Pinterest trends, and presentation minimums and maximums, along with supply chain constraints, such as vendor minimums and costs, create an optimal inventory level and purchase quantity. When retailers leverage an analytical optimization process, they create an accurate plan that is derived in an efficient manner and aligns with the buyers' workflow. This process ensures that customers find the right product to drive them to purchase.

However, in order for the customer to purchase, the right style in the right color has got to be available in the right size. Retailers can leverage advanced imputation techniques to account for missed opportunities in demand. Imputation is an analytical approach to processing missing data. In this case, our missing data is the miss in sales due to the fact that the store did not have the inventory in stock. Advanced techniques decipher where in the product life cycle these stock-outs took place in order to truly maximize profitable demand. Retailers are much more concerned with a stock-out in the first week of the product life cycle than in the last week when markdowns are taking place.

Allocation is the process of planning out how much each store or fulfillment center will receive of each item in the assortment. Understanding how customers are shopping helps retailers to intelligently allocate and fulfill. As customers come to expect free shipping, retailers must cut down on shipping costs to drive profitability while ensuring that customers have a seamless shopping experience. Leveraging advanced allocation models that take into account a store's total need for a classification or subclassification as well as demand (which is determined by a statistical forecast) ensures that the right product gets to the right place and at the right time.

If a size is not available in-store, customers expect a seamless experience across channels. The ability to order from a kiosk in-store, on a mobile app, or online and pick up in-store are examples of leveraging an omnichannel strategy so that customers have the flexibility to shop in whatever way they choose and still experience the same level of convenience and satisfaction. An omnichannel strategy also creates tension and challenges for retailers to accurately predict demand by channel and plan inventory in line with the demand as customers move more toward online purchases and online ordering with in-store pickup. Leveraging a statistical forecast to project demand by channel is an approach for retailers in addition to advanced allocation and fulfillment models.

To truly determine the right location for fulfilling online orders, data is needed on which stores have excess unproductive inventory, as well as geolocation information to minimize shipping costs and which store can fulfill the largest number of items, among others. Retailers can leverage customer data that gives insights into how customers are shopping and then what channels are being used to further understand and plan fulfillment strategies for the future. Taking advantage of optimization, retailers are able to utilize analytics to find the optimal scenario and fulfillment location to deliver the goods to the customer in the most convenient yet economical manner for the retailer. These key activities enhance customers' experience throughout their journey and drive customers to further purchases in the future.

Determining how customers shop—in-store, online, or picking up in-store—enables retailers to best ensure that the right product is in the right place at the right time. Optimal fulfillment strategies provide seamless customer journeys and drive profitability by reducing shipping costs. Each piece in the process is an integral and connected step. Without a strategic merchandise financial plan, a retailer's assortment plan would not be in line with the higher-level trends of the business. Without a customer-centric assortment, the customer would not be able to find the items that were desired, regardless of the sizes. Without the proper sizes, the customer would not be able to purchase, regardless of how in line the assortment is with his or her preferences. Without a proper allocation, the inventory would not be in the right place at the right time. Without the proper fulfillment strategy, retailers would lose a great deal of money in shipping fees in order to maintain a seamless customer journey between channels. It is critical that the customer is in the center of each of these steps.

Retailers manage their assortment from financial plan to breaking that plan down to an assortment plan and then optimizing by size. They leverage allocation and fulfillment strategies to get the right product to the right store or customer at the right time. Once these steps in the process have been done, the next step is managing the pricing life cycle, as discussed in Chapter 5. Determining the right ticket or regular price preseason is the first step in the pricing life cycle. Once the item has arrived in the stores and begins to sell in-season, promotional pricing can be utilized to drive through inventory. Promotions drive traffic for retailers but also cost them once prices are reduced. Leveraging analytics, retailers can understand what the most effective promotional pricing should be in order to be the most strategic. Price elasticity is a statistical analysis that gives insight into what items, customer segments, or store locations are the most sensitive to a drop in demand when price fluctuations occur.

Understanding customers and how they respond to price enables retailers to manage assortments most strategically throughout the season and to the end of the merchandise life cycle, when items are being marked down to clearance. Understanding what levers drive customers' path to purchase enables retailers to be more strategic in planning promotions. Different promotional vehicles that can be utilized include a percentage off, a dollar amount off the price, or a buy one get one free. These types of vehicles can lead to personalized pricing online and in-store. Buyers can leverage this type of process to sell through inventory that may be excess while still achieving their gross margin goals. These efforts are also tied to marketing, which is the overall strategic planning, execution, and measurement of how a retailer or a brand interacts with its customers and how that brand is perceived. Marketing has become a lifetime relationship between a brand and a customer.

Retailers leverage analytics as well as customer insight into price sensitivity to determine in season how best to promote products to drive through inventory and gain incremental margin. Without the right product, marketing becomes pointless. Retailers use customer intelligence to gain insight into their customers. A central data source that presents a 360-degree perspective on the customer enables retailers to understand what customers are buying, how they are buying it, their online behavior, and their use of social media. Having this information on customers enables retailers to personalize pricing and messaging to truly grow the relationship. Marketers can communicate these promotional strategies that connect the overall promotional activity for the total store along with item-level promotions to connect customers to what truly interests them and would drive them to purchase. Marketers communicate with customers through mobile apps and utilize proximity marketing through those mobile apps to communicate with customers when they are near local stores. They use clienteling techniques in-store.

Marketers utilize analytical segmentation to group together similar customers to personalize at a customer level. Even though customers may be segmented together, each customer must feel that the communication between him or her and the retailer is personalized. Key aspects to driving a customer's lifetime value are making the customer feel that the information that is communicated is relevant to them and that the retailer is communicating in the most effective way, whether that is e-mail, text message, or direct mail. Their lifetime value is the projected profitability that a retailer will gain from the customer over the lifetime of the relationship. Effective communication also supports the customer journey.

Along the journey, customers must feel safe and protected. Customers expect retailers to safeguard them from becoming victims of credit or debit card theft, which occurs through data breaches. Cybersecurity measures have been put in place to protect customers. Regulation and standards from the payment card industries have forced retailers to utilize these standards. Ensuring that personal information is stored safely is critical. New technology has also been advanced to include Europay, Mastercard, and Visa (EMV) chip cards. On credit and debit cards, magnetic strips contain the sensitive information. Fraudsters use card skimmers to copy this information after the magnetic strips are swiped. Chip cards minimize criminals' ability to make copies of cards to use in fraudulent purchases. Machine learning and predictive analytics alert and predict which suspicious activities are malicious and fraudulent. When or where these activities occur and items that are most likely to be fraudulently purchased can be predicted as well. Retailers have to be proactive instead of reactive to protect customers throughout the journey and to ensure that customers can move seamlessly throughout the different shopping channels. Customers have to feel that they can safely make purchases on a retailer's website if the retailer is executing an omnichannel strategy and providing a true customer journey.

CHAPTER 10

Millie and Boomer: Generations Unified

We have walked through how retailers leverage analytics to solve business challenges in Chapters 1 through 9. Two additional aspects to successfully leveraging analytics in an organization are the people and the process. As generations shift, it becomes imperative to understand how these different generations (people) perceive technology and how to drive change (process).

When I first started my career in retail, there was a clear line between generations. "Millennial" is a term that refers to anyone born between the 1980s and 2004. A baby boomer is anyone born from 1946 to 1964. These individuals grew up in completely different worlds. Millennials grew up when technology was just starting to become mainstream. Most millennials had computers throughout high school, and cell phones and Internet access was available 24/7 when they started their first jobs. The baby boomer generation worked their first careers without computers, cell phones, Internet, or e-mail. They grew up in an era when communication was in person and careers were 9-to-5 jobs. They looked for companies they could work at until retirement and had a strong loyalty to their employers.

Millennials are quickly taking over the workforce just as they are becoming an increasing percentage of retail consumers. We spoke in Chapter 3 about the challenges retailers face learning how best to curate assortments that meet millennials' merchandise preferences. Millennials tend to be driven to purchase more experiences than material objects. They are also more about individualism in style and less about conforming to a logo or brand image. They are driving retailers to move from being product centric to becoming customer centric. As customers, millennials are changing retailers' historic business approaches. But they are also changing and affecting retailers as employees. Millennials are projected to be 50% of the workforce by 2020 and 70% of the workforce by 2030.

Millennials have grown up in a world of technology. They have learned on laptops and tablets. You hardly ever see a student with a notebook in a college lecture anymore. It is all laptops. Technology has been infused into their education and is a key component of their personal lives through social media and being continuously connected to the web via an average of three devices. Younger generations will be even more involved with technology early on. The best video I have seen that reflects the changing behaviors is one where a toddler is given a magazine. The little girl starts to swipe the magazine, not understanding that pages must be turned because she is so accustomed to swiping her mother's iPad.

Because of their lifestyle, millennials have a very hard time adapting to business processes that include paper reports, notebooks, desktop computers, and green screen computer systems, which are terminals that display a black screen with green characters, to do their job. These methods are completely archaic to millennials. To stay in the retail game, to increase their competitive advantage, and also to retain and attract top talent, retailers need to infuse analytics and technology into their processes. Millennials do not want to perform a mundane task that could be automated through software, and they know what capabilities are out there. Even retail and fashion colleges or programs are incorporating analytics into their education programs.

On the flip side, the baby boomer generation presents completely different challenges. These individuals grew up taking notes the old-fashioned way; toting a laptop to type in a meeting feels unnatural to many of them. These baby boomers are also at the brink of retirement. The youngest baby boomer in 2020 will be 56. In 2016, baby boomers retired at a rate of 10,000 per day, and two out of three college graduates will land a job as a result of baby boomers retiring. Analytics become critical as millennials become a greater proportion of the workforce along with the complexities of understanding the millennials and the changing retail marketplace.

At the same time, these two generations can complement each other's strengths and weaknesses. When it comes to implementing a more analytical business process in retail, millennials tend to be much more responsive. They were raised with STEM (science, technology, engineering, and mathematics) education. Millennials can become very strong change agents for a company and can partner with employees who are stuck in their own ways. Often certain employees feel that they have been doing things the same way for 20 years and there is no need to change. These individuals do not see how the retail environment is changing so rapidly that old ways just do not cut it; neither do they think about tackling the future.

For millennials and baby boomers to work together successfully, they have to recognize the value of the other and leverage each other's strengths. Millennials have much to learn from older generations, who have worked for far longer. They have seen economic downfalls and have learned how to analyze, understand, and react to them. They have had both successes and failures and have learned from each. Baby boomers understand the concept of doing more with less. They understand the repercussions of economic downfalls and have learned from history. They have a strong work ethic and loyalty to their employers. These individuals can tell war stories for days.

At the same time, millennials can also offer knowledge to baby boomers. These millennials, including myself, have learned how to really create a work–life balance. They have learned how to work flexibly so that they can still enjoy a meaningful life, including a social and family life. Historically, retail corporate offices had an 8-to-5 work schedule. However, it was expected that workers came into the office at 7 and stayed until 7. Leaving earlier than that reflected negatively on employees' work ethic, which in my opinion is just crazy. It should not matter if you are working at your desk, via your cell phone, or at home. It is all about getting the job done, not how long it takes to get the job done. Millennials are all about working smarter. This is why analytical and automated processes to perform mundane tasks are a key benefit to millennials. They would much rather be doing something more meaningful to the company than a repetitive task and then be able to leverage analytics to think about new ways to change the business or new ideas to test. This is also why it is critical to have an analytical business process that supports working remotely. Remote access to environments or cloud offerings is key to supporting the business anywhere, anytime, in any way.

Millennials have learned to think outside the box, becoming creative and innovative. Older generations often become set in their ways. Molding the next generations into individuals who are not afraid of change, who look forward to trying new things, and who are coming up with ideas to move toward the future is key to driving business growth in such a competitive marketplace. These individuals, whether business users, citizen data scientists that were discussed in Chapter 11, or data scientists, can take a challenge and strategically determine how best to solve a problem. Business users may offer a conceptual explanation. Citizen data scientists can interpret this business conceptual process to data scientists in a way that statistically explains the vision. Then data scientists can create analytical processes to solve these challenges.

Millennials are also extremely resourceful. If they don't know something, they know how to find the answer. Their natural instinct is to Google anything they do not know. They know what sites to go to in order to find relevant information. They leverage their social network extensively. Millennials are a generation of "phone a friend" but through text and social network connections, connections that are intertwined into their lives. Baby boomers also are extremely connected. Baby boomers have a long history of creating personal connections and relationships. Retail is a small world, and everyone knows someone who knows someone. These generations just are connected in different ways. Hand a millennial a business card, and he or she will most definitely snicker. Instead, they will connect online through LinkedIn, Twitter, or Facebook. Millennials are a digitally connected generation. They want receipts e-mailed to them, if at all. They want e-mails, not snail mail. They want paperless billing. It's all about having access to information 24/7. If I have your business card, then I must remember to take it with me in order to connect with you. Why in the world would I do that when I could have contact information in the phone that I have with me 24/7? Understanding how to react and best communicate with different personalities and work or management styles is an important skill. Often technologically driven communication paths do not seem to be effective. E-mails can be read or interpreted incorrectly or taken personally. Baby boomers can help to put that emotion and personal relationship building into the equation. When implementing a different business approach, users want to know that their feelings and thoughts matter. Users want to feel like part of the decision-making process when any business process is being changed.

I remember going through a team-building exercise early in my career where everyone on our team took a personality test that asked various questions related to what I would do in a certain situation, how I feel, and how I would react. Based on responses, the test grouped individuals in four quadrants. The y-axis illustrated the taskmaster characteristics and the x-axis illustrated the socializer.

I was a hard-core taskmaster. This made so much sense as I read the description of a taskmaster. It was like I was reading my own bio. My boss at the time was in the complete opposite quadrant. As I read the description for that quadrant, it fit exactly as well. I realized that the characteristics we differed in complemented our working partnership. In the emotional arena, I was low in sensitivity, but I was strong in getting the job done. With this realization, I was able to be much more self-aware and work on becoming a stronger leader. But it also showed me that one person cannot be everything. That is why we are not all walking around like robots with the exact same mentality, attitude, and style. But the concept of supporting two types of people's strengths with the other's weaknesses and vice versa is truly how we work together and become successful. One person's strength in an area can complement another coworker's weakness. This same type of mentality can be applied to different generations as well. We all bring something unique to the table.

When it comes to ensuring that each individual's thoughts and concerns matter, millennials are not afraid to speak up and take risks, regardless of whether it is accepted or not. This concept is definitely different between generations, and I think each generation balances each other out here. Most of the time, reading the audience can give insight into the degree to which a person speaks their mind. Many baby boomers grew up in an era when high-level executives were the thought leaders and lower-level team members did not disagree, as that could have been interpreted as disrespectful. This situation has definitely changed. Creating a culture where employees feel supported to speak their opinion is important in change management. When implementing any kind of solution or analytical process in the retail industry, it is very important to the success of the project to include user feedback, regardless of the user's level in the organization, keeping in mind the time, place, and audience. Often executives are so removed from day-to-day tasks of managing the business that end users may be able to shed light on and voice a concern that wouldn't have been considered until a major problem arose. Millennials and baby boomers can take notes from each other to have a successful project.

Millennials are job hoppers. Baby boomers often frown on this characteristic, but looked at from a positive perspective, millennials know that in order to work their way up and earn more, they must hop around. Don't get me wrong; there is a fine line between meaningful job hopping and unreliability. Moving every five years is completely acceptable. Moving every year, not so much. But the acceptable transitions have enabled millennials to learn different approaches, different processes, different systems, and different ways of thinking about the business. These millennials are quickly moving up in the ranks and have learned to leverage their different experiences to create a best-of-breed approach. Rising millennials can lean on the lengthy experience and deep-rooted understanding of a baby boomer's perspective on a retailer.

It is important to understand how the generations must mix. As customers, millennials have had a direct impact on retailers. They also have had a direct impact as key employees, influencers, and decision makers. Attracting and retaining top talent now and in the future will include a retail environment that leverages analytical insights in the business process, automated approaches to increase efficiencies, and give these individuals the opportunity to truly stretch their creativity, innovation, and forward thinking to move companies to the next level of innovation. Flexibility in work–life balance is also essential to drive innovation as we continue to live in a fully connected world where both work and personal life commingle just as generations do.

CHAPTER 11

How to Gain Personal Value from Analytics

Whether you are just starting out your career and looking to educate yourself on analytics or are a seasoned veteran who wants to understand how things are changing and what the future of retail will look like, you can gain value from learning and leveraging analytics. Throughout this book, we have discussed the importance of leveraging analytics in the retail process, from creating strategic plans, curating assortments, fulfilling inventory, pricing, and marketing to the in-store experience and cybersecurity. Each component benefits from analytics by increasing accuracy and efficiencies and enabling a more personalized engagement with customers. As the digital landscape continues to evolve and competition is at an all-time high, analytics become critical for retailers to stay in the game.

At the same time, art is a large component of retail. Style and fashion are both forms of art, personal art. Retail cannot be completely mathematical or black and white. Analytical insights are a part of retail merchandising, pricing, marketing, in-store experience, and cybersecurity. However, an understanding of the customer, an eye for taste and art, and a deep understanding of the business and strategy are critical to truly leverage an analytical approach.

"Domain knowledge" is a term that describes having knowledge related to the customer, the business, and the strategy. There will never be a day when you walk into a retail corporate office and it is 100% statisticians. Buyers are typically hired for their eye for fashion and taste, not because they have PhDs in statistics. Marketers typically have a great sense of business strategy and vision. Store associates are brought on because of their ability to connect with customers. These business users need to be able to leverage analytics, and the insights must be consumable and easy to understand so that the users can move from insight to action.

This is where the concept of approachability comes into play. Often, if you mention analytics to business users or buyers, they look at you like a deer frozen in headlights. The key to a successful analytics-based process is approachability. Visualization is a popular method of reporting and of showing analytical insights in easy-to-understand ways. Analytical insights can be visualized in the form of line graphs, bar charts, pie charts, bubble plots, heat maps, and many graphic forms. Through visualizations, business users can personally leverage analytical insights into their day-to-day work lives. Regardless of your analytical skill set, visualizations are used to interpret the results in a way that makes sense for business users so that you can gain value from them. For example, we discussed using regression analysis to determine which attributes are most important to customers' purchasing decisions in Chapter 3. The results of regression analysis can be visualized in a pie chart showing the importance of each attribute as a percentage contribution.

Visualization has almost become the norm in analytical software in the market. The actual core analytics that are presented vary significantly by software vendor, depending on their maturity in the analytical market and their expertise. But anyone can make a pie chart. Analytical insights must also be aligned with workflow. Analytics or any software solution works best when it is integrated into users' day-to-day normal working habits. If the first thing buyers do when determining the assortment is to determine the overall choice count needed, this first step in their workflow should remain consistent. What would change is the core determination of the choice count. Instead of looking at historical numbers, for example, buyers would be presented with optimized figures determined through analytics or visualizing the difference on a bar chart.

Reporting visualizations by themselves is not practical. We often use the term "operationalizing the analytics" to describe the ability to actually take the analytical insights and apply them to a work function. The insights are not just nice to know; how can users take action on this information? And is this information in an easy-to-use form, so users do not necessarily need to read a report and then manually make decisions in a separate tool? The process must be integrated and seamless for true adoption and efficiency. So in our example, the choice count can be visualized but also placed as the starting working values in buyers' actual assortment planning worksheets. One-off reports are not always practical for short-staffed departments. Sure, some retailers start off with integrating analytical insights as reports offered to the business as they begin to infuse analytics into their current process, and this can be very beneficial. But to get the complete package, integration is key. Having an analytical process integrated into the workflow will enable you to do your job more efficiently, and your results will be more accurate. Typically, retail employees are reviewed each and every year on their job performance. Additional business key performance indicators are also used to review employees. For example, merchandise planners typically are graded on their sales, gross margin performance, and inventory turn or some type of productivity metric. Having a statistical forecast to predict sales enables you to have a more accurate sales plan. This in turn gets you closer to your end-of-year goals, which most times will result in a bonus, raise, or possibly promotion. Not only can you gain from analytics, making your job easier by visualizations and integrated workflow, these analytics help drive your personal career success.

CITIZEN DATA SCIENTIST

To understand how best to visualize this information for the end business user, you must understand the analytics. You need to have a strong understanding of what the analytics are actually doing in order to translate that into visualizations and explain them in layman's terms for business users who are questioning results. But again, you also must have the domain knowledge to understand what exactly the business is trying to achieve, what the strategic initiatives are, how analytics can be leveraged, and what the best approach should be. The term "citizen data scientist" was coined by Gartner, an analyst firm, in 2015; it describes an individual who sits right in the middle of the art and the analytics.

Often, this role has been positioned as a liaison between the business and the analytics teams and the information technology (IT) team. Citizen data scientists can clearly articulate the business challenges, needs, wants, and requirements. These individuals can also clearly articulate to businesses what the approach is and how it will solve their challenges or fulfill their requirements. There was initially a bit of a stir over this exact term. Hard-core data scientists felt almost insulted that people without their level of expertise could be placed in a similar arena. I personally think the hard-core data scientists were being prima donnas. Today the general concept of citizen data scientists is very much accepted in the industry as people who bring together business domain knowledge and understanding of the analytics.

If you currently have domain knowledge and are interested in learning more about analytics, the citizen data scientist is a great path for you. This path is also a great fit if you have a strong understanding of analytics but would like to gain more knowledge about retail business or if you are just starting your career and envision yourself as a combination of Einstein and Picasso. I suggest starting out by taking an introductory statistics course focused on business. A great way to find these courses is through analytical software companies. These training classes are geared more toward solving real-world business problems. Over the years, I have found that this approach helps me learn in more depth because the material is explained more easily in the form of a business challenge or scenario. The SAS Institute offers many training classes in analytical approaches related to business problems. These classes are hands-on rather than lectures. They also have training paths so you have a good guide into what class to take next, and each class builds on the previous one.

If you have this type of training, either on the job or through your college experience, but you would like to learn more about retail, I suggest you look for a position at a corporate retail office. One of the best ways to get a variety of experiences is through management training programs, which many retailers offer. These programs typically create rotations where employees work in various positions in the corporate office. For example, a trainee may spend four months in merchandise planning, four months in merchandise buying, four months as a store manager, and four months in marketing. Throughout these rotations, trainees attend weekly or biweekly meetings to hear special guests speak about their jobs and different components of the industry.

This experience is extremely beneficial as it helps to create a sense of how all pieces truly do fit together. The best part of this process is being on the other side of the desk when one task creates complications downstream. For example, say trainees go through their allocation rotation before their buying rotation. Often these trainees have to key in purchase orders during their buying rotation. In other words, the trainees are given purchase order spreadsheets and must key the information into the merchandising system. If trainees key the order incorrectly, it would create additional work once the purchase order came to the distribution center for allocation. The analyst would have to call the buying office to make the adjustment and then resend the allocation. During my time in a management trainee program, it was interesting to watch trainees cope with the annoyance of calling the buying office and having to have them resend the allocation. After trainees moved to the buying rotation, they would key in their orders with 100% accuracy. Because they understood how important it was to get it right the first time, they paid extra attention. Individuals who work through management training program rotations graduate with a better sense of the process and understanding how one task on one side of the business affects the other areas of the business.

CHANGE AGENT

Whether it is learning more about analytical approaches through further training or understanding how to tackle business challenges through hands-on practical experience, moving toward a strong understanding of both sides is a great approach to gaining personal value from analytics. Citizen data scientists are in high demand, and the demand will continue to grow as analytical approaches to tackling the ever-changing retail environment increase. These individuals are also key in system implementations. That is actually how I first realized my love for technology and analytics. I was nominated by my company's president to be a part of my company's allocation software implementation. These implementations typically involve a solution design workshop, where business teams get together with software consultants to talk about the current challenges and the future vision of a process. After these workshops, the consulting team can tailor the solution or analytics to fit the process. Once the solutions and/or analytics are tailored to fit the future vision, the next step is testing to make sure that it works, that the results are what is expected, and that the workflow is also aligned; this is called user acceptance testing. A key to success in both these steps is participation and speaking up.

Being a part of an implementation team can be a lot of fun and a lot of pressure. You are the voice for the entire user community, which is why it is critical to speak up and not be afraid to have an opinion. Chances are that if you are thinking something, other people on the team are thinking the same thing, and the user community would agree as well. Being an implementation team member is a great way to further your career and development. You learn a lot about yourself and how to work well with a team. You learn that you have many strengths that you may not have recognized.

Being a member of an implementation team also enables you to learn the solution and gain deeper understanding of the business. Learning how certain aspects of a workflow affect downstream elements is also beneficial. In order to test the system, you have to think of every way possible that users would try to use the solution as well as every business scenario. Thinking outside the box on how you might tackle a specific business problem that may not be inherent in the solution is also a great way to exercise your creativity. Once the acceptance testing is complete, then the solution roll-out occurs.

You become the change agent. You are the champion for the solution and help others to understand the solution, how it works, and its benefits. Having a strong change management process and team is critical to successful implementations. Often analytics is thought of as a black box from the user community. The term "black box" is used to describe the lack of understanding of what the analytics are actually doing and how the analytics are coming up with the results. This is why it becomes critical for change agents and/or citizen data scientists to be able to explain how specific analytics work and the results in a way that is easy for users to understand. You can have the best software out there, but if the user community does not accept it, it does no good. System implementations are always about having the people, the process, and the technology. Retailers must have all three, which is why becoming the change agent for a retailer can be very beneficial to your success. Most times when a software implementation is occurring to gain analytical insights and efficiencies, people fear their positions are at risk. Typically if retailers expect to gain efficiencies and no longer need some of their staff, they will look to move these individuals elsewhere in the business and have them focus on driving the business forward rather than performing mundane tasks that can now be automated. Enhanced collaboration and vision generation are also key benefits to being able to move individuals across the organization. Rarely are these individuals fired, but sometimes it does happen.

Individuals often fear change and the idea of becoming superfluous. This can create a massive amount of apprehension and hinder the adoption process during an implementation. These individuals need to be assured that their jobs are not at risk. This is where having upper management supporting the project and communicating the future vision is vital. The adoption and support must come all the way from the top of the company, including the C-suite.

The support of the change agents is also required. Communication that the process includes the technology and the people drives the success of the implementation. Just as we have discussed throughout this book, retail requires the merging of art and analytics. It is the people who bring the true art of retail along with the deep understanding of customers as well as their business strategies such as growing national brands versus private label or changing the pricing strategy from being nonpromotional to offering promotions and coupons. Becoming the change agent for a retailer enables you to become the leader in the success of the business. The change agent is the go-to person for the user community when they have questions or issues arise.

I encourage individuals who are looking to move to becoming change agents or citizen data scientists in their organizations to offer or volunteer to be on a project. Any chance to get involved with technological changes is a great way to learn more and find out if this type of career is for you.

FINDING THE RIGHT FIT

You might also be starting out early in your career and have not yet found a retailer. If this is the case, I encourage you to interview a retailer just as much as you are being interviewed. Do your homework. At the end of the day, you want to find a retailer that enables you to grow with the company, regardless of your current career level. Looking for a retailer that aligns with your style of work and management is critical as well. For example, if you are looking for a work environment that offers flexibility, such as flexible hours, then make sure you ask the questions. Work–life balance is a very important element. I have found this to be very true as I balance working and being a mom. I want the flexibility to have an extremely successful career but also not miss my son's school plays or Muffins with Mom on Mother's Day. This flexibility continues to become the norm across organizations as perceptions of flexibility and connectedness change.

It also is important to find a career where you can continue to learn and evolve. Management training programs are a great way to learn across how the entire business functions or if you just aren't sure which aspect of the business resonates the most with you. Does the retailer offer continuous learning and training? Is there tuition reimbursement if you are looking to continue to expand your knowledge? These are great questions to ask when interviewing to find the right fit for you.

Technology is also an important aspect to understand. Are you looking to become a change agent at a retailer, or are you looking for a retailer that already has advanced technology set in place that you'd like experience with? Many times you can learn a lot about what type of technology retailers use by reading their job descriptions. A list of job descriptions, including positions in IT, can give insight into what skills the retailer is look for. These descriptions or skills needed may include Excel and PowerPoint but also may list specific software experience, such as SAS. This type of research can give insight into the types of tools the retailer leverages. System administrator roles also typically show these software solutions under "desired skills." As technology advances, you want a clear understanding of what type of systems retailers have today and what their plans or visions for the future are. If technology and learning more about analytics is important to you, the last thing you want to do is land a job at a retailer that is still using green bar reports and ancient, homegrown solutions. The work may end up being extremely mundane and repetitive due to a lack of automation.

Last, you want to ensure that you will be able to learn and grow in your role and have a clear understanding of your career path for the future. Sometimes retailers may have a very tough promotion process. Promotions may be hard to come by, and future growth and movement may be slim to none. You may find this type of an organization in rural areas where there is little competition. These retailers are the only game in town, and therefore employees do not leave or move on to other opportunities. The only time a position becomes available is when someone retires or dies. In contrast, in New York City, people are continuously moving around in the industry, and positions are available quite frequently. This is something to take note of and be cautious. One way to get a sense of the potential for personal growth is by talking to people you know who work at the retailer and looking at their LinkedIn profiles to see their movement over the years.

THE VALUE OF ANALYTICS

This book has emphasized that analytics can help retailers to drive profitability. Throughout the entire retail business, analytical insights can be infused into the merchandising, pricing, marketing, in-store experience, and cybersecurity divisions to connect retailers to customers. Customers are at the forefront of each step in the process. Our first step in the process was creating high-level merchandise financial plans by using statistical forecasts that capture changes in demand by product and by channel to ensure market trends are incorporated into the financial strategy.

Then we discussed breaking these higher-level merchandise plans down to item-level assortment plans to begin to curate the product offerings that tie to customers' merchandise preferences. We were able to cluster our locations as well as trade areas based on a statistical clustering approach rather than traditional sales volume and/or climate-based assortments. Doing this helps in further localizing the product offerings based on customer demand, moving away from product-centric assortments to customer-centric assortments. We leveraged analytical insights to understand which products were driving the business and the risks and opportunities while taking into account additional data elements, such as social media and spatial constraints. From there, we were able to understand and predict trends by leveraging merchandise attributes and combinations of attributes that were not even in the assortment to identify missed opportunities. Then these item-level assortments were further broken down to the size level based on the true size demand, taking into account if the store out-of-stocks as where in the product life cycle these out-of-stocks occurred. Retailers are moving forward by creating profitable, localized assortments down to the size level to ensure the product is in the right place at the right time to drive sales and reduce markdowns while leveraging analytics.

From there, analytics are used to determine the right price to drive the customer to purchase and enable retailers to gain incremental margin throughout the product life cycle. These assortments and pricing strategies are then used in conjunction with marketing efforts to ensure the most relevant price, product, and promotional type is being presented to customers, whether through e-mail, direct mail, texts, or notifications via the retailer's app. Leveraging analytics, retailers can be more strategic in their marketing spending and increase their return on investment. Strategically understanding which customers are most likely to respond to an offer or which ones would purchase items regardless of the promotion drives profitability.

We can then further refine this communication and path to purchase in-store by leveraging real-time data and advanced technology in the Internet of Things. Being able to support clienteling and connecting further with customers to grow customer loyalty and purchase sizes drive sales and market share. We can then protect customers by utilizing analytics in cybersecurity initiatives. This not only protects customers from having their personal information stolen but also protects retailers from data breaches and resulting financial impacts.

Throughout each step, analytical capabilities are utilized to create more efficient processes. Increased efficiencies enable end users to focus on driving the business forward with collaboration and vision generation. These efficiencies create a better work environment where employees are not wasting time on boring, mundane tasks. These analytical capabilities are also driving the success of the business throughout any of these steps in the process, and each end user is rewarded based on performance and business success. Leveraging analytics to drive the key performance indicators enables analytics to be used for your own personal gain.

In 2018, the industry demand for people who are skilled in analytics could outpace the number of users by 60%. This equates to 1.5 million new jobs. Further growing your own skill set and knowledge as it relates to the business and analytical aspects are key ways to drive your career forward. Citizen data scientists who aid users in understanding what the analytics are doing and what is going on is a rapidly growing career path. These individuals often are hard to come by, so their salaries can be very competitive. An article by Monster.com stated that SAS was the number one skill to lead to a larger paycheck. Learning how to interpret analytical insights and enhancing your analytical skill set by learning SAS code can help you advance in your career. Students can leverage this skill set to land great jobs right out of school, and retailers can leverage SAS to attract top talent.

Whether you are coding, becoming a change agent in an implementation, are a citizen data scientist, or are an end user who wants to grow your knowledge, it is critical to learn and grow your understanding of analytics. When it comes to leading as a change agent, being able to communicate to the end user these elements enables adoption and change management. Without successful adoption and change management, a retailer could spend millions of dollars and not gain a return on investment. Whether you are looking for a position in merchandising, pricing, marketing, or in-store or cybersecurity, there are opportunities to pursue and expand your knowledge.

Continue to educate yourself by signing up for a training class. SAS.com offers free tutorials and training classes across the United States and globally. These classes are taught both hands-on and remotely and give you practical applications to test and grow your knowledge. You can take a basic business knowledge class, where the conceptual information is taught. Advanced analytical programming courses are also available, such as regression analysis and predictive modeling. Courses are offered to educate individuals on software solutions; the Statistical Forecast Studio offers users a graphical user interface.

Continue reading books to grow your knowledge set. Further your education by taking college courses, or think about pursuing a master's degree. Download free software. SAS University Edition offers free SAS software to students, who can download the software and learn hands-on in the comfort of their own homes. Take charge of your success and learn how to leverage analytics. If you are currently in school, take an analytical course or ask if there are any courses that teach SAS. YouTube is another great channel to continue education. There are a wealth of recorded trainings and seminars. SAS has its own YouTube channel with a library of videos to educate viewers; there are even product demonstrations.

If you are currently working at a retailer, SAS also offers a try-before-you-buy program for its Visual Analytics, the SAS visualization and reporting tool. Users of this tool can visualize and report analytical insights via pie charts, line graphs, bubble plots, and many more formats. This tool also offers the ability to pull in word clouds from Twitter, Google Analytics, and Facebook. Multiple data sources are supported, including SAS data sets, Excel spreadsheets, CSV files, SAP HANA, and many more. I encourage you to test drive this tool via the SAS website at www.sas.com.

The SAS communities also have a plethora of information and share programming code, ask questions, and discover additional capabilities. Demonstration videos and code snippets are accessible to share among users. SAS has a very strong community and support network. SAS also offers a user-led conference known as SAS Global Forum. Each year, users from all over the globe and from many industries meet together for workshops, keynote addresses, and user-led presentations. At these conferences, users can learn what's new at SAS and collaborate with others and stay forward thinking into the future.

SAS makes it its mission to ensure that the user community has a voice and is included in advancing technologies. SAS reinvests 25% of its revenue each year in research and development to move forward into the future as industries and demands change.

I encourage you to continue to move forward by continuously educating yourself on SAS offerings and capabilities. Speak up in your career. Leverage analytics to get your foot in the door, land your dream job, and benefit your current position within the company as well as your future career growth. Challenge the norm. Most important, drive change for the future and have fun doing it! You may find that you are artistically inclined and envision yourself becoming that fabulous designer who will sketch out and create products. You might find you love the excitement and hustle and bustle of working in stores. Taking down hackers and stopping cyberattacks might sound like the ultimate battle for you. Working with creative teams to craft beautiful marketing campaigns and flyers to collaborate with merchants on trends and events along with understanding relevant customer communication might lead you down a marketing path. Or envisioning a career of shopping for your assortment to tie to your customer as a merchant or buyer may appeal as the dream job. There truly is a place for each and every person in the wonderful world of retail. In every aspect, you can drive the future with analytics.

References and Resources

REFERENCES

Deloitte. "Omni-Channel Retail, A Deloitte Point of View." February 2015. https://www2.deloitte.com/content/dam/Deloitte/se/Documents/technology/Omni-channel-2015.pdf.

Greg Girard, Leslie Hand, Spencer Izard, and Miya Knights. "IDC Future-Scape: Worldwide Retail 2015 Predictions." https://www.idc.com/getdoc.jsp?containerId=252327.

Holt, Jeff. "A Summary of the Primary Causes of the Housing Bubble and the Resulting Credit Crisis: A Non-Technical Paper." *Journal of Business Inquiry* 8, no. 1 (2009): 120–129. https://www.uvu.edu/woodbury/docs/summaryoftheprimarycauseofthehousingbubble.pdf.

Kesteloo, Marco, and Nick Hodson. "Bricks & Clicks: 2015 Retail Trends." strategy &. http://www.strategyand.pwc.com/perspectives/2015-retail-trends.

Koehn, Nancy F. "The History of Black Friday." Marketplace Commentary, American Public Media, November 25, 2011. http://www.marketplace.org/2011/11/25/life/commentary/history-black-Friday.

Lunka, Ryan. "Retail Data: 100 Stats About Retail, eCommerce & Digital Marketing." nChannel. https://www.nchannel.com/blog/retail-data-ecommerce-statistics/.

Pfeuffer, Charyn. "Job Skills That Lead to Bigger Paychecks." http://www.monster.com/career-advice/article/best-paid-job-skills.

Neosperience Team. "10 Useful Customer Experience Statistics for Your 2015 Strategy." December 12, 2014. http://blog.neosperience.com/10-useful-customer-experience.

Nielsen. "The Sustainability Imperative: New Insights on Consumer Expectations," October 2015. http://www.nielsen.com/content/dam/nielsenglobal/dk/docs/global-sustainability-report-oct-2015.pdf.

Ray, Tiernan. "Amazon 'Becoming Fashionable,' Says Morgan Stanley; 20% Apparel Share by 2020?" Tech Trader Daily, May 12, 2016. http://blogs.barrons.com/techtraderdaily/2016/05/12/amazon-becoming-fashionable-says-morgan-stanley-20-apparel-share-by-2020/.

ReferencesCMO Council. "Marketing Spend." https://www.cmocouncil.org/facts-stats-categories.php?view=all&category=marketing-spend.

Sorin, Kay. "Luxury Department Stores Use Fashion Bloggers to Attract Consumers." *Luxury Daily*, February 23, 2015. https://www.luxurydaily.com/fashion-bloggers/.

US Bureau of Labor Statistics. "Databases, Tables and Calculators by Subject." http://data.bls.gov/timeseries/LNS14000000.

RESOURCES

"Demand-Based Store Clustering by Example with SAS Enterprise Miner: Part 1," SAS Communities Library, December 18, 2015. https://communities.sas.com/t5/SAS-Communities-Library/Demand-Based-Store-Clustering-by-Example-with-SAS-Enterprise/ta-p/239768.

SAS, Training & Books/Training, http://support.sas.com/training/tutorial/.

SAS, Visual Analytics, http://www.sas.com/en_us/software/business-intelligence/visual-analytics.html.

SAS, Retail Analytics: Better Retail from Better Analytics, http://www.sas.com/en_us/industry/retail.html.

Schafer, Lori, and Bernard Brennan. *Branded! How Retailers Engage Consumers with Social Media and Mobility*. Hoboken, NJ: John Wiley & Sons, 2010.

Glossary

Aggregation

The sum or collection of data. Often "aggregation" is used to summarize sales at various levels of the merchandise, location, and time hierarchy.

Allocation

The process of distributing inventory to retail locations and fulfillment centers in an effort to fulfill future customer demand, whether it is in-store or online.

Assortment

Term used to describe the product offerings carried by a retailer. These product offerings vary based on location clusters and whether for e-commerce or brick-and-mortar sites.

Assortment planning

The curation of the array of merchandise assortment that is offered to the customer, along with planning key performance indicators, such as planned demand and inventory productivity. Typically assortment plans are created at the location cluster level in order to localize and create customer-centric assortments.

Attribute

A characteristic of a hierarchical level. Attributes are used to describe levels of the merchandise and location hierarchy.

Beacon technology

A form of the Internet of Things. Beacon technology consists of small chips that utilize Bluetooth low energy signals to communicate with other devices. iBeacon is a specific beacon technology for Apple products.

Big data

Large sets of data that are leveraged to make better business decisions. Retail data can be sales, product inventory, e-mail offers, customer information, competitor pricing, product descriptions, social media, and much more.

Brick and mortar

Term used to describe the physical store locations of a retailer.

Bulk

Product that comes in multiples of ones.

Cannibalism
The concept that items may hurt or reduce the demand of other items or take away demand when these items are on promotion. For example, a buy one get one free promotion of one brand may reduce the demand for a brand that is not on sale.

Casepacks
Term used for products that are delivered to retailers in packs of multiple sizes. For example, a retailer will receive a specific style in a defined color in packs where each pack includes 1 small, 2 mediums, 2 large, and 1 extra-large. This is often referred to as a 1-2-2-1 casepack.

Center moving average
The representation of a typical sales volume centered on a specific level of time.

Channel
Term used to describe the mechanism by which customers shop and retailers connect with the customers. These channels include, but are not limited to, in-store, online, catalog, call center, mobile apps, social media, and others.

Chargeback
A payment retailers are required to pay to customers when fraudulent purchases are made to refund the fraudulent activity. Retailers usually must pay chargebacks when customers do not receive the product or did not make the charge. Each time a purchase is flagged as fraudulent, the retailer must refund the money to the victim.

Citizen data scientist
Term coined by Gartner, an analyst firm, that describes an individual who sits in the middle of the art and analytics. This individual has a firm understanding of analytics to be able to explain and interpret them to business users but also understands the business itself and has domain knowledge.

Complex casepack
Term that describes when products are delivered to retailers in packs of multiple items and multiple sizes. For example, one complex casepack includes a specific style of dress in a defined color, along with a top and a bottom. Each item is also packed to include 1 small, 2 mediums, 2 large, and 1 extra-large. Complex casepacks are efficient ways to deliver collections and/or season setups.

Contextual marketing
Refers to strategically marketing relevant products and promotions to customers based on their specific preferences and browsing behavior.

Cookies
Text files that store customers' browsing behavior and track their movement on websites in the users' browser directories. The information is anonymous but is leveraged for web profiling and contextual marketing.

Cost
The price a retailer has to pay the vendor for items.

Customer
An individual who has previously purchased or will one day purchase items from a retailer.

Customer centric
The concept of putting customers in the center of importance and determining product assortment decisions based on how customers are reacting to these merchandise attributes. Historically, retailers have been more product centric and chose the products that would dictate what customers would buy.

Customer intelligence
Knowledge related to a retailer's customers to better communicate and drive purchases. By collecting this intelligence or knowledge through data, retailers can better understand customers and, in turn, personalize and grow the relationship. Customer intelligence leverages all data, including real-time data, to create one single view of customers and performs analytics on this data to gain insight in order to react and engage quickly with customers.

Customer journey
A term that describes the seamless process of interacting with the retailer across multiple channels, which include, but are not limited to, in-store, online, catalog, call center, mobile apps, and social media.

Customer lifetime value
A measurement of how much profit a retailer will retain over the lifetime relationship with a specific customer. This measurement is often leveraged to understand who the most valuable customers are in an effort to become more strategic with marketing efforts.

Customer loyalty programs
Rewards programs that retailers offer to customers to give special promotions, sneak peeks at new products, and even points or cash back on purchases to incent customers to shop more frequently and increase the purchase size and dollar amount.

Customer relationship management
A solution that enables retailers to store data about their customers. This data is typically static, such as customer records, sales, and interactions with the call center.

Customer segmentation
Grouping together customers based on similar shopping preferences, shopping behavior, demographic information, and promotional effectiveness. Customer segmentation is leveraged in multiple aspects of the retail business to more efficiently drive personalization while driving the most strategic and cost saving processes for the retailer. Clustering customers into segments gives insight into similar shopping preferences, which retailers use to understand which customers have similar profiles, what products should be targeted, and what promotional and marketing vehicles drive the highest return on investment for each segment of customers.

Cyberattack
When electronic data is used without authorization or malicious activities occur, such as spyware and viruses.

Cybersecurity
The ability to protect against the unauthorized use of electronic data and malicious activity. This electronic data can be personal customer information such as names, addresses, social security numbers, credit cards, and debit cards, to name a few.

Database
A set of data contained in a location on a network, computer, or server. Typically, different data sets are stored in different databases. Examples of these databases include inventory, selling price point, and sales, divided into total dollar sales and unit sales.

Data governance
The security of data as well as its availability to users. Data governance ensures that employees are not able to access confidential data and data they do not need during their day-to-day jobs.

Data mining
Term used to describe analyzing large amounts of data to find patterns, correlations, and similarities.

Demand transference
The understanding of how demand could cross over between similar categories or correlated categories.

Deseasonalizing data
The process of removing the seasonality from historical demand values. This type of approach is used during time-series decomposition in an effort to capture price effects.

Deterministic approach
An approach to targeting customers that determines whether a user is associated with a device ID. A marketer associates a device ID with customers once they specifically log in to their account on the retailer's site from the device. The deterministic approach is much more accurate and widely used than the probabilistic approach.

Domain knowledge
A term that describes having knowledge related to the customer, the business, and the strategy.

Dynamic hierarchy
Also referred to as alternate hierarchies, it is a hierarchy that is created outside of the standard hierarchy. It leverages attributes to define and re-organize the data.

EMV
Credit and debit card technology that stands for Europay, Mastercard, and Visa, companies that were the creators of these cards. The cards contain a chip. To make a transaction, users place the card into a chip reader instead of swiping the magnetic strip. The chip contains encrypted credit card or debit card information along with customer information. The encrypted code changes each time the card is utilized in a transaction. Chip card transactions also require a PIN or signature, which makes it very difficult for hackers to steal account and credit/debit card information to re-create cards for fraudulent purchases.

Event-stream processing
Term that describes the action of taking specific actions or events in real time and processing them to supply an outcome, which may be an action.

Fiscal
Of or related to government revenue or taxes.

Fulfillment
Term that refers to the process of meeting a customer's specific order need.

Gross margin
Money made when you take the total dollar sales of an item and/or level of the hierarchy and subtract what that item cost.

Gross margin percentage
Percentage of profit earned from sales.

Hierarchy
Ranking system where items are classified into different levels. Three hierarchies are utilized in a merchandising hierarchy perspective: merchandise, location based, and time. People in retail refer to this as MLT (merchandise, location, and time).

iBeacons
Technology that Apple created and has incorporated into Apple devices to communicate with each other and send alerts and messages. This technology is a subset of beacon technology.

Imputation
Process of replacing missing data with values. Imputation is utilized in optimizing sizing of the assortment to replace missing sales data due to a lack of inventory.

Internet of Things
Also referred to as IoT. Term that describes the connectivity of objects to the Internet and the ability for these objects to send and receive data from each other.

IP address
Each device that customers use to surf the Internet has an associated Internet Protocol (IP) address. This IP address is a set of unique numbers that represents the device.

Key performance indicators
Most frequently referred to as KPIs. Metrics that indicate the performance of the business.

Logistic regression
Form of regression analysis where the dependent variable is a category rather than a continuous variable. An example of a continuous variable

is sales or profit. In order to understand customer retention, regression analysis would calculate the effects of variables such as age, demographics, products purchased, and competitor information on two categories: retaining the customer and losing the customer.

Machine learning
Computer programs that have the ability to learn over time as new data becomes available. This type of analytical programming can learn more about a customer's online shopping behavior over time and start to predict which items the customer will likely click on and purchase.

Malware
Software created to steal information or corrupt the hardware.

Markdown cadence
Determination of the schedule and price point of the initial clearance price as well as any additional price reductions.

Markdown price
Last stage of a merchandise life cycle. Very few items are left, and they are typically merchandised on the floor in a specific area. Some refer to this as clearance or a clearance zone.

Market basket analysis
Analysis that looks at historical point-of-sale data by transaction to understand which items are most frequently bought together.

Marketing
Overall strategic planning, execution, and measuring of how a retailer or a brand interacts with its customers and how that brand is perceived. Public relations and community involvement aid in brand perception. Marketing has become a lifetime relationship between a brand and a customer.

Marketing automation
Automating the strategic targeting of customers based on their merchandise preferences, the marketing vehicles that most influence them and drive them to purchase, and the value of those customers. There may be two segments of customers or a multitude of segments so it is important for retailers to have a way to automate the targeting process and repeat in the future.

Merchandise financial planning
Creating a financial plan at levels of the merchandise, location, and time (MLT) hierarchy. These plans are created to better understand the

business, react to trends, find risks and opportunities, and quickly react or course correct. Merchandise planners create a financial and strategic plan that includes key performance indicators (KPIs).

Millennials

Term used to describe people who were born between the years 1982 and 2004. This generation has predominantly grown up during the age of technology and is projected to comprise 70% of the workforce by 2030.

Omnichannel

Means by which retailers and consumers engage with each other across touchpoints through one seamless customer experience. It's truly a plethora of touchpoints, including in-store, website, mobile site, mobile apps, Snapchat, Twitter, Pinterest, Instagram, Facebook, YouTube, and Amazon. The term "digital landscape" is also used for this mix of channels.

On order

Inventory that is on its way or planned to be received.

Optimization

Term used to describe analytics that calculate and determine the most ideal scenario to meet a specific target. Optimization procedures analyze each scenario and supply a score. An optimization analytic can run through hundreds, even thousands, of scenarios and rank each one based on a target that is being achieved.

Path to purchase

Term that describes how customers interact with different channels to ultimately purchase items from a retailer. These channels can include Google Searches, e-mail campaigns, mobile apps, websites, and social media ads on Facebook, Pinterest, and Instagram, to name a few.

Payment Card Information Data Security Standard

Known as PCI DSS. Standards put in place to protect storage and handling of customer payment card information (PCI).

Phishing

Term that describes when an attacker poses as someone else or an actual company to gain confidential information.

Probabilistic approach

Cross-identifying customers with device IDs leveraging analytical models to predict and associate a customer to a specific device ID, a numeric and character value to distinguish individual devices.

Product centric
Concept that buyers were focused on what products they carried and brought to the market rather than what customers were looking for.

Promotional price
Price of the item that helps drive sales and traffic. These prices are temporary price reductions and can fluctuate. Often these promotional pricing strategies occur in-season as retailers are reacting to demand and inventory concerns.

Proximity marketing
The process of leveraging location to deliver marketing. A mobile device is an Internet of Things object that receives a signal when the device is near the source location. Proximity marketing can be in the form of local advertisements.

Real-time data
Term that refers to the availability of data as soon as that data is collected. Access to real-time data can be leveraged for pricing decisions as well as marketing to drive actions.

Receipts
Unit and dollar amount of inventory that is needed to get back up to the ideal inventory necessary to drive profitable sales.

Reconciliation
Term that describes the different levels of the hierarchy meeting at intersections.

Regular price
Price on the item ticket. In retail, this is typically a price that is not changed once the product reaches the store. This price is also determined before the season begins.

Retargeting
Tracking a user's online activity through cookies. Although the information is anonymous, it can be used by advertisers, who buy this information and create advertising spots directed at customers based on what items or types of items they have browsed.

Retention
The ability to keep customers over time and avoid losing them as customers.

RFM model
A modeling technique that gives retailers insight into which customers are the most valuable or the ability to determine customer lifetime value.

RFM stands for recency, frequency, and monetary. Recency pertains to how recently the customer made a purchase. Frequency represents how often the customer makes purchases at the retailer. Monetary represents the profitability associated with the customer over time.

Seasonality
Pattern that is predictable, such as the Christmas holiday season, as well as nonholiday predictable sales lifts and declines.

Sentiment
Emotion or feeling that is portrayed through text data.

Sentiment analysis
Analyzing unstructured data, such as text data, for emotion. Often this analysis is represented in the form of a positive sentiment, a negative one, or a neutral one.

Showrooming
Concept of customers leveraging brick-and-mortar locations to see, touch, and feel the product but purchasing via mobile apps or websites.

Shrinkage
Discrepancies between actual inventory on hand and tracked inventory due to theft, wastage, and damages.

Size scale
Term that describes the quantity that retailers should buy of each style-color by size as well as how much each location should receive.

Skimmers
Reading devices that criminals use to steal credit and debit card information, much like hackers attacking point-of-sale systems but on a smaller scale.

Statistical forecasting
Analytical process to predict future values. In retail, statistical forecasting leverages historical sales to predict future demand. These sales are typically patterns. These patterns can contain five main components: seasonality, trend, events, causal factors, and outliers. Historical sales can contain one of these components, a combination, or even all five.

Stock to sales
Analyzing the size performance contribution compared to the inventory ownership contribution.

Store clustering
Grouping retail stores based on similarities, such as volume or climate, or on more advanced analytical techniques, such as similar selling patterns.

Structured data
Information that sits in a database, file, or spreadsheet. It is generally organized and formatted. In retail, this data can be point-of-sale data, inventory, product hierarchies, or others.

Third-party data source
Company that collects data and sells it to retailers, such as demographic information for local areas.

Time-series decomposition
Concept that suggests that data makeup consists of trends, seasonality, and irregular patterns. These irregular patterns can be caused by factors such as promotions.

Trade area
Geographic area surrounding a store location. If you were to look on a map of where a store is located, the surrounding area is typically where the majority of the customers reside.

Trade area characteristics
Insights that describe a specific trade area, such as the average income, age, population, and ethnicity.

Transaction
Each individual purchase. Each time customers swipe a card, shell out cash, or press the purchase confirmation button online, a transaction takes place. This data often is referred to as transaction log (T-log) data.

Unstructured data
Data that does not have a specific format. It can be customer reviews, tweets, pictures, or even hashtags.

Vendor minimums
Minimum buy quantities that merchants must meet in order to sell the product.

Weeks of supply
Number of weeks it would take to sell all of the inventory.

Retail Math

Formulas are taken from Retail Math Formulas, About Money, http://retail.about.com/od/retailingmath/a/retail_formulas.htm.

Average Inventory (Month) = (Beginning of Month Inventory + (PE) End of Month Inventory) ÷ 2

Retail Price = Cost of Goods + Markup

Markup = Retail Price − Cost of Goods

Cost of Goods = Retail Price − Markup

Cost of Goods Available = Beginning Inventory + Purchases − Ending Inventory

Gross Margin = Total Sales − Cost of Goods

Gross Margin Return on Investment = Gross Margin $ ÷ Average Inventory Cost

Initial Markup % = (Expenses + Reductions + Profit) ÷ (Net Sales + Reductions)

Turnover = Net Sales ÷ Average Retail Inventory

Markdown % = $ Markdown ÷ $ Net Sales

Margin % = (Retail Price − Cost) ÷ Retail Price

Markup $ = Retail Price − Cost

Markup % = Markup Amount ÷ Retail Price

Sales per Square Foot = Total Net Sales ÷ Square Feet of Selling Space Sell Through

Sell Through % = Units Sold / (Units + On-Hand Inventory)

Shrinkage = Difference between Book and Physical Inventory

Stock-to-Sales = Beginning of Month Stock ÷ Sales for the Month

Weeks of Supply = On-Hand Inventory at Retail ÷ Weekly Sales at Retail

Index